KB043836

Reading Schedule

이 책은 총 29,200개의 단어로 구성되어 있습니다.(중복 포함, 1페이지는 대략 145단어)
분당 150단어 읽기는 원어민이 말하는 속도입니다. 먼저 이 기준을 목표로 시작해보세요.

● 1회 읽기

날 짜	/	/	/	/	/
시 간	~	~	~	~	~
페이지	~	~	~	~	~

내용 이해도 ☑ 90%이상 ☑ 70% ☑ 50% ☑ 30%이하

리딩속도 계산 [200] ÷ [   ] X [145] = [   ]

전체 페이지　　　　시간(분)　　　1페이지 당 평균 단어수　1분당 읽은 단어수

● 2회 읽기

날 짜	/	/	/	/	/
시 간	~	~	~	~	~
페이지	~	~	~	~	~

내용 이해도 ☑ 90%이상 ☑ 70% ☑ 50% ☑ 30%이하

리딩속도 계산 [200] ÷ [   ] X [145] = [   ]

전체 페이지　　　　시간(분)　　　1페이지 당 평균 단어수　1분당 읽은 단어수

● 3회 읽기

날 짜	/	/	/	/	/
시 간	~	~	~	~	~
페이지	~	~	~	~	~

내용 이해도 ☑ 90%이상 ☑ 70% ☑ 50% ☑ 30%이하

리딩속도 계산 [200] ÷ [   ] X [145] = [   ]

전체 페이지　　　　시간(분)　　　1페이지 당 평균 단어수　1분당 읽은 단어수

식은 죽
먹기야~

● 전체 평가

체감 난이도 ☑ 상 ☑ 상중 ☑ 중 ☑ 중하 ☑ 하

읽기 만족도 ☑ 나는 리딩의 고수!

☑ 좀 잘했군요~

☑ 노력하세요.

☑ 난 머리가 안 좋나봐 -.-;

꿀벌 마야의 모험

리딩 속도가 빨라지는 영어책 012

꿀벌 마야의 모험
The Adventures of Maya the Bee

2017년 6월 10일 초판 1쇄 인쇄
2017년 6월 20일 초판 1쇄 발행

지은이 발데마르 본젤스
발행인 손건
편집기획 김상배, 홍미경
마케팅 이언영
디자인 김지영
제작 최승용
인쇄 선경프린테크

발행처 LanCom 랭컴
주소 서울시 영등포구 영신로 38길 17
등록번호 제 312-2006-00060호
전화 02) 2636-0895
팩스 02) 2636-0896
홈페이지 www.lancom.co.kr

ISBN 979-11-88112-14-2 13740

꿀벌 마야의 모험

The Adventures of Maya the Bee

발데마르 본젤스 지음

LanCom
Language & Communication

꿀벌 마야의 모험 줄거리

　태어난 지 하루 만에 동료들을 따라 꿀을 모으러 처음
으로 바깥 세계에 나온 아기 꿀벌 마야는 자연의 아름다
움에 이끌려 바로 모험의 세계에 뛰어든다.

　넓디넓은 바깥 세상은 어두운 꿀벌 도시보다 천 배는
더 좋을 것이라고 생각하면서 평생 꿀이나 모으고, 밀랍
으로 집이나 지으며 살지는 않겠다고 결심한 것이다.

　호기심 많은 마야는 꽃이 만발한 온 세상을 구경하면서
자유롭게 마음 내키는 대로, 이끌리는 대로 세상 곳곳을
돌아다닌다. 장미 꽃 속에 사는 풍뎅이를 만나고, 난생
처음 보는 호수를 하늘이라 착각한다.

　하늘처럼 눈부신 호수 위에 떠있는 연잎 위에서 우연히
금파리를 만나 이야기를 나누다가 금파리가 눈앞에서 잠
자리에게 잡아먹히는 것을 목격하게 된 마야는 그 끔찍
한 장면에 치를 떨다가도 어느덧 잠자리의 투명한 날개
며 그 멋진 모습에 매혹된다.

　귀뚜라미 에피를 사랑하는 딱정벌레 바비를 있는 힘
을 다해 도와주고, 사방으로 뛰어다니는 메뚜기며, 인간
을 잘 안다고 떠벌리는 집파리 푸크를 만나 새로운 사실
들을 알아가던 어느 날 마야는 거미줄에 갇히게 된다. 하
지만 마음을 다해 도와주면 그 도움은 다시 돌아오는 법,
마침 지나가던 딱정벌레 바비가 목숨을 구해준다.

지독한 냄새를 풍기는 노린재 때문에 질겁하는 마야를
보고 웃어대는 나비한테 화를 내다가도 어느새 또 그 아
름다운 모습에 넋을 잃고 마는 마야.

　어느 날 한밤중에 눈을 뜬 마야는 처음으로 낮과는 전
혀 다른 밤 세상을 구경하면서 감탄하고 감동한다. 처음
보는 달빛, 고요한 숲속, 차가운 대기, 모든 것이 신기하
고 낯설고 아름답다. 그 밤에 마야는 꽃의 요정을 만나
그토록 간절히 보고 싶어 하던 인간을 만나게 된다.

　그렇게 온갖 일을 겪으며 돌아다니다가 마야는 말벌의
포로가 된다. 절망 속에서 죽음을 기다리던 마야는 자기
일족을 습격하려는 말벌들의 계획을 엿듣게 된다. 모험
심 강하고 용감하고 긍정적이며 자부심 강한 마야는 자
기 일족이 멸망을 앞두고 있다는 사실에 괴로워한다. 자
기 일족에 대한 격렬한 사랑, 충성심, 그리움에 사무친
마야는 일족을 구하기 위해 있는 힘을 다해 탈출한다.

　고향을 향한 필사적인 비행으로 마침내 고향에 돌아온
마야는 여왕벌에게 위험을 알린다.

　마야는 용감하고 대담하고 비범한 여왕의 모습에 감탄
한다. 치열한 전투 속에서 수많은 사상자가 났지만 여왕
의 뛰어난 전술과 지략으로 꿀벌들은 말벌들을 물리친
다. 믿을 수 없는 꿀벌의 승리, 있을 수 없는 말벌의 패
배! 슬픔과 애도 속에서도 꿀벌들은 바로 일상으로 돌아
가고 마야는 여왕의 친구가 된다.

CONTENTS

1

FIRST FLIGHT

The elderly lady-bee who helped the baby-
나이 지긋한(eld는 old보다 정중한 표현)
bee Maya when she awoke to life and
(잠에서) 깨다[깨우다] (AWAKE의 과거)
slipped from her cell was called Cassandra and
벌방   (이름이) ~인: ~라 불리는
commanded great respect in the hive. Those
(응당 받아야 할 것을) 받다   존경(심), 경의   벌집: (한 벌집에 사는) 벌떼
were exciting days. A rebellion had broken out
신나는, 흥미진진한, 흥분하게 하는   반란   ~이 발생하다[터지다]
in the nation of bees, which the queen was un-
국가: (한 국가의 전체) 국민
able to suppress. While the experienced Cas-
(정부, 통치자 등이) 진압하다   경험이 풍부한: 능숙한
sandra wiped Maya's large bright eyes and tried
(물기를) 닦다[훔치다]
as best she could to arrange her delicate wings,
정리하다, 배열하다   연약한, 여린, 다치기 쉬운
the big hive hummed and buzzed like a threat-
웅웅[붕붕]거리다   위협적인 천둥번개
ening thunderstorm, and the baby-bee found it

very warm and said so to her companion.
동반자, 동행: 친구[벗]

Cassandra looked about troubled, without replying. It astonished her that the child so soon found something to criticize. But really the child was right: the heat and the pushing and crowding were almost unbearable. Maya saw an endless succession of bees go by in such swarming haste that sometimes one climbed up and over another, or several rolled past together clotted in a ball.

Once the queen-bee approached. Cassandra and Maya were jostled aside. A drone, a friendly young fellow of immaculate appearance, came to their assistance. He nodded to Maya and stroked the shining hairs on his breast rather nervously with his foreleg. The bees use their forelegs as arms and hands.

"The crash will come," he said to Cassandra. "The revolutionists will leave the city. A new queen has already been proclaimed."

Cassandra scarcely noticed him. She did not even thank him for his help, and Maya felt

keenly conscious that the old lady was not a bit
날카롭게 의식하는
nice to the young gentleman. The child was a
little afraid to ask questions, the impressions
(~로부터 받는) 인상[느낌]
were coming so thick and fast; they threatened
잇따라 대거; 시시각각으로 벌어지는
to overwhelm her. The general excitement got
(격한 감정이) 휩싸다[압도하다]   흥분; 흥분되는 일
into her blood, and she set up a fine, distinct
맑은   뚜렷한, 분명한
buzzing.
윙윙거리다

"What do you mean by that?" said Cassandra.

"Isn't there noise enough as it is?"
소음, 시끄러운 소리

Maya subsided at once, and looked at Cassan-
가라앉았다, 진정되다
dra questioningly.
질문조로, 미심쩍게, 수상하다는 듯이, 왜 그러냐는 듯

"Come here, child, we'll see if we cannot

quiet down a bit." Cassandra took Maya by her

gleaming wings, which were still soft and new
빛나는, 환한
and marvelously transparent, and shoved her
놀라울 만큼[불가사의하게, 믿을 수 없을 만큼] 투명한
into an almost deserted corner beside a few

honeycombs filled with honey.
벌집   ~으로 가득 채워지다

Maya stood still and held on to one of the

cells.

"It smells delicious here," she observed. Her
맛있는   관찰[관측/주시]하다: 지켜보다
remark seemed to fluster the old lady again.
정신을 못차리게 하다; 당황하게 하다

11

"You must learn to wait, child," she replied. "I have brought up several hundred young bees this spring and given them lessons for their first flight, but I haven't come across another one that was as pert and forward as you are. You seem to be an exceptional nature."

Maya blushed and stuck the two dainty fingers of her hand in her mouth.

"Exceptional nature—what is an exceptional nature?" she asked shyly.

"Oh, *that's* not nice," cried Cassandra, referring not to Maya's question, which she had scarcely heeded, but to the child's sticking her fingers in her mouth. "Now, listen. Listen very carefully to what I am going to tell you. I can devote only a short time to you. Other baby-bees have already slipped out, and the only helper I have on this floor is Turka, and Turka is dreadfully overworked and for the last few days has been complaining of a buzzing in her ears. Sit down here."

Maya obeyed, with great brown eyes fastened
on her teacher.

"The first rule that a young bee must learn,"
said Cassandra, and sighed, "is that every bee,
in whatever it thinks and does, must be like the
other bees and must always have the good of all
in mind. In our order of society, which we have
held to be the right one from time immemorial
and which couldn't have been better preserved
than it has been, this rule is the one funda-
mental basis for the well-being of the state. To-
morrow you will fly out of the hive, an older bee
will accompany you. At first you will be allowed
to fly only short stretches and you will have to
observe everything, very carefully, so that you
can find your way back home again. Your companion will show you the hundred flowers and
blossoms that yield the best nectar. You'll have
to learn them by heart. This is something no bee
can escape doing.— Here, you may as well learn
the first line right away—clover and honeysuck-

le. Repeat it. Say 'clover and honeysuckle.'"

"I can't," said little Maya. "It's awfully hard. I'll see the flowers later anyway."

Cassandra opened her old eyes wide and shook her head.

"You'll come to a bad end," she sighed. "I can foresee that already."

"Am I supposed later on to gather nectar all day long?" asked Maya.

Cassandra fetched a deep sigh and gazed at the baby-bee seriously and sadly. She seemed to be thinking of her own toilsome life—toil from beginning to end, nothing but toil. Then she spoke in a changed voice, with a loving look in her eyes for the child.

"My dear little Maya, there will be other things in your life—the sunshine, lofty green trees, flowery heaths, lakes of silver, rushing, glistening waterways, the heavens blue and radi-ant, and perhaps even human beings, the high-est and most perfect of Nature's creations. Be-

14

cause of all these glories your work will become
a joy. Just think—all that lies ahead of you, dear
heart. You have good reason to be happy."

"I'm so glad," said Maya, "that's what I want
to be."

Cassandra smiled kindly. In that instant—
why, she did not know—she conceived a peculiar
affection for the little bee, such as she could not
recall ever having felt for any child-bee before.
And that, probably, is how it came about that
she told Maya more than a bee usually hears on
the first day of its life. She gave her various spe-
cial bits of advice, warned her against the dangers of the wicked world, and named the bees'
most dangerous enemies. At the end she spoke
long of human beings, and implanted the first
love for them in the child's heart and the germ
of a great longing to know them.

"Be polite and agreeable to every insect you
meet," she said in conclusion, "then you will
learn more from them than I have told you to-

day. But beware of the wasps and hornets. The
hornets are our most formidable enemy, and
the wickedest, and the wasps are a useless tribe
of thieves, without home or religion. We are a
stronger, more powerful nation, while they steal
and murder wherever they can. You may use
your sting upon insects, to defend yourself and
inspire respect, but if you insert it in a warm-
blooded animal, especially a human being, you
will die, because it will remain sticking in the
skin and will break off. So do not sting warm-
blooded creatures except in dire need, and then
do it without flinching or fear of death. For it
is to our courage as well as our wisdom that
we bees owe the universal respect and esteem
in which we are held. And now good-by, Maya
dear. Good luck to you. Be faithful to your people and your queen."

The little bee nodded yes, and returned her
old monitor's kiss and embrace. She went to
bed in a flutter of secret joy and excitement and

16

could scarcely fall asleep from curiosity. For the
거의 …않다; 겨우, 간신히 　　　　　호기심

next day she was to know the great, wide world,
큰, 위대한　넓은

the sun, the sky and the flowers.

　　Meanwhile the bee-city had quieted down.
그 동안에, 그 사이에　　　　　　평정을 되찾다, 조용해지다

A large part of the younger bees had now left
leave의 과거·과거분사

the kingdom to found a new city; but for a long
왕국　　　　　　　　　　　　　오랫동안, 장기간

time the droning of the great swarm could be
윙윙거리는　　　(한 방향으로 이동하는 곤충의) 떼[무리], 벌 떼

heard outside in the sunlight. It was not from

arrogance or evil intent against the queen that
오만, 교만, 거만　　　의지, 의향(intention): 목적, 계획

these had quitted; it was because the population
(살던 곳을) 떠나다　　　　　　인구, (모든) 주민

had grown to such a size that there was no

longer room for all the inhabitants, and it was
(특정 지역의) 주민[서식 동물]

impossible to store a sufficient food-supply of
불가능한, 대단히 곤란한, 난감한　　충분한 식량 공급

honey to feed them all over the winter.
밥[우유]을 먹이다: 먹이를 주다

　　You see, according to a government treaty of
~에 의하면; ~에 따라　　　　　　조약, 계약

long standing, a large part of the honey gathered
오래된, 전통 있는

in summer had to be delivered up to human be-
인도하다; 되돌려주다; (성 따위를) 넘겨주다

ings, who in return assured the welfare of the
(~에 대한) 보답[답례]으로　　(개인, 단체의) 안녕[행복]

bee-state, provided for the peace and safety of
제공[공급]하다, 주다

the bees, and gave them shelter against the cold
(비, 바람, 위험 등으로부터) 막아 주다

in winter.

17

"The sun has risen!"

The joyous call sounding in Maya's ears
아주 기뻐하는; 기쁜, 기쁨을 주는; 쾌활한
awoke her out of sleep the next morning. She

jumped up and joined a lady working-bee.
일벌

"Delighted," said the lady cordially. "You may
다정하게, 진심으로
fly with me."

At the gate, where there was a great push-
가득 모여 밀치며 바글거리다
ing and crowding, they were held up by the
붙잡히다
sentinels, one of whom gave Maya the password
보초병, 감시병   암호를 알려주다
without which no bee was admitted into the
들어가다, 입장하다
city.

"Be sure to remember it," he said, "and good
(명령문으로 쓰여) 꼭[반드시] ~을 해라
luck to you."

Outside the city gates, a flood of sunlight
쇄도, 폭주, 홍수
assailed the little bee, a brilliance of green and
공격을 가하다. (몹시) 괴롭히다   광휘; 광명, 광택
gold, so rich and warm and resplendent that she
눈부시게 빛나는[멋진]
had to close her eyes, not knowing what to say

or do from sheer delight.
순전한, 순수한
"Magnificent! It really is," she said to her
참으로 아름다운. 너무나 감명 깊은. 굉장히 훌륭한
companion. "Do we fly into that?"
동반자, 동행
"Right ahead!" answered the lady-bee.

Maya raised her little head and moved her pretty new wings. Suddenly she felt the flying-board on which she had been sitting sink down, while the ground seemed to be gliding away behind, and the large green domes of the tree-tops seemed to be coming toward her.

Her eyes sparkled, her heart rejoiced.

"I am flying," she cried. "It cannot be anything else. What I am doing must be flying. Why, it's splendid, perfectly splendid!"

"Yes, you're flying," said the lady-bee, who had difficulty in keeping up with the child. "Those are linden-trees, those toward which we are flying, the lindens in our castle park. You can always tell where our city is by those lindens. But you're flying so fast, Maya."

"Fast?" said Maya. "How can one fly fast enough? Oh, how sweet the sunshine smells!"

"No," replied her companion, who was rather out of breath, "it's not the sunshine, it's the flowers that smell.— But please, don't go so fast, else

I'll drop behind. Besides, at this pace you won't observe things and be able to find your way back."

But little Maya transported by the sunshine and the joy of living, did not hear. She felt as though she were darting like an arrow through a green-shimmering sea of light, to greater and greater splendor. The bright flowers seemed to call to her, the still, sunlit distances lured her on, and the blue sky blessed her joyous young flight.

"Never again will it be as beautiful as it is to-day," she thought. "I *can't* turn back. I can't think of anything except the sun."

Beneath her the gay pictures kept changing, the peaceful landscape slid by slowly, in broad stretches.

"The sun must be all of gold," thought the baby-bee.

Coming to a large garden, which seemed to rest in blossoming clouds of cherry-tree, hawthorn, and lilacs, she let herself down to earth, dead-tired, and dropped in a bed of red tulips, where she held on to one of the big flowers. With a great sigh of bliss she pressed herself against the blossom-wall and looked up to the deep blue of the sky through the gleaming edges of the flowers.

"Oh, how beautiful it is out here in the great world, a thousand times more beautiful than in the dark hive. I'll never go back there again to carry honey or make wax. No, indeed, I'll never do that. I want to see and know the world in bloom. I am not like the other bees, my heart is meant for pleasure and surprises, experiences and adventures. I will not be afraid of any dangers. Haven't I got strength and courage and a sting?"

She laughed, bubbling over with delight, and took a deep draught of nectar out of the flower of the tulip.

"Grand," she thought. "It's glorious to be alive."

21

Ah, if little Maya had had an inkling of the
many dangers and hardships that lay ahead of
her, she would certainly have thought twice. But
never dreaming of such things, she stuck to her
resolve.

Soon tiredness overcame her, and she fell
asleep. When she awoke, the sun was gone,
twilight lay upon the land. A bit of alarm, after
all. Maya's heart went a little faster. Hesitatingly
she crept out of the flower, which was about
to close up for the night, and hid herself away
under a leaf high up in the top of an old tree,
where she went to sleep, thinking in the utmost
confidence:

"I'm not afraid. I won't be afraid right at the
very start. The sun is coming round again; that's
certain; Cassandra said so. The thing to do is to
go to sleep quietly and sleep well."

2

THE HOUSE OF THE ROSE

By the time Maya awoke, it was full day-light. She felt a little chilly under her big green leaf, and stiff in her limbs, so that her first movements were slow and clumsy. Clinging to a vein of the leaf she let her wings quiver and vibrate, to limber them up and shake off the dust; then she smoothed her fair hair, wiped her large eyes clean, and crept, warily, down to the edge of the leaf, where she paused and looked around.

The glory and the glow of the morning sun were dazzling. Though Maya's resting-place still

lay in cool shadow, the leaves overhead shone
like green gold.

"Oh, you glorious world," thought the little
bee.

Slowly, one by one, the experiences of the
previous day came back to her—all the beauties
she had seen and all the risks she had run. She
remained firm in her resolve not to return to the
hive. To be sure, when she thought of Cassandra, her heart beat fast, though it was not very
likely that Cassandra would ever find her.— No,
no, to her there was no joy in forever having to
fly in and out of the hive, carrying honey and
making wax. This was clear, once and for all.
She wanted to be happy and free and enjoy life
in her own way. Come what might, she would
take the consequences.

Thus lightly thought Maya, the truth being
that she had no real idea of the things that lay in
store for her.

Afar off in the sunshine something glimmered
멀리에, 멀리 떨어져, 까마득히

red. A lurking impatience seized the little bee.
도사린   성급함: 조급, 안달, 초조, 조바심

Moreover, she felt hungry. So, courageously,
게다가, 더욱이   용감하게, 대담하게

with a loud joyous buzz, she swung out of her
윙윙거림: 윙윙[옹옹]거리는 소리

hiding-place into the clear, glistening air and the
숨어 있던 곳[장소]   반짝이는

warm sunlight, and made straight for the red
따뜻한   일직선으로[곧장] 나아가다

patch that seemed to nod and beckon.
(주변과는 다른 조그만) 부분   (오라고) 손짓하다. (손짓으로) 부르다

When she drew near she smelled a perfume
향기, 향내

so sweet that it almost robbed her of her senses,
털다[도둑질하다]

and she was hardly able to reach the large red
겨우, 간신히   닿다. 도착하다

flower. She let herself down on the outermost of
가장 바깥쪽의

its curved petals and clung to it tightly.
꽃잎   cling(꼭 붙잡다. 매달리다)의 과거, 과거분사

At the gentle tipping of the petal a shining

silver sphere almost as big as herself, came roll-
구체; 구슬   ~만큼 큰   굴러오다

ing toward her, transparent and gleaming in all
~쪽으로   투명한   반짝이는

the colors of the rainbow. Maya was dreadfully
무지개빛으로   몹시, 굉장히

frightened, yet fascinated too by the splendor
겁먹게[놀라게] 만들다   마음을 사로잡다. 매혹[매료]하다   훌륭함, 화려함

of the cool silver sphere, which rolled by her,
차가운 은빛 구슬

balanced on the edge of the petal, leapt into the
균형을 유지하다[잡다]   leap의 과거, 과거분사

sunshine, and fell down in the grass.
떨어지다

Oh, oh! The beautiful ball had shivered into a score of wee pearls. Maya uttered a little cry of terror. But the tiny round fragments made such a bright, lively glitter in the grass, and ran down the blades in such twinkling, sparkling little drops like diamonds in the lamplight, that she was reassured. She turned towards the inside of the calix. A beetle, a little smaller than herself, with brown wing-sheaths and a black breastplate, was sitting at the entrance. He kept his place unperturbed, and looked at her seriously, though by no means unamiably.

Maya bowed politely.

"Did the ball belong to you?" she asked, and receiving no reply added: "I am very sorry I threw it down."

"Do you mean the dewdrop?" smiled the beetle, rather superior. "You needn't worry about that. I had taken a drink already and my wife never drinks water, she has kidney trouble.— What are you doing here?"

"What is this wonderful flower?" asked Maya, not answering the beetle's question. "Would you be good enough to tell me its name?"

Remembering Cassandra's advice she was as polite as possible.

The beetle moved his shiny head in his dorsal plate, a thing he could do easily without the least discomfort, as his head fitted in perfectly and glided back and forth without a click.

"You seem to be only of yesterday?" he said, and laughed—not so very politely.

Altogether there was something about him that struck Maya as unrefined. The bees had more culture and better manners. Yet he seemed to be a good-natured fellow, because, seeing Maya's blush of embarrassment, he softened to her childish ignorance.

"It's a rose," he explained indulgently. "So now you know.— We moved in four days ago, and since we moved in, it has flourished wonderfully under our care.— Won't you come in?"

Maya hesitated, then conquered her misgivings and took a few steps forward. He pressed aside a bright petal, Maya entered, and she and the beetle walked beside each other through the narrow chambers with their subdued light and fragrant walls.

"What a charming home!" exclaimed Maya, genuinely taken with the place. "The perfume is positively intoxicating."

Maya's admiration pleased the beetle.

"It takes wisdom to know where to live," he said, and smiled good-naturedly. "'Tell me where you live and I'll tell you what you're worth,' says an old adage.— Would you like some nectar?"

"Oh," Maya burst out, "I'd love some."

The beetle nodded and disappeared behind one of the walls. Maya looked about. She was happy. She pressed her cheeks and little hands against the dainty red hangings and took deep breaths of the delicious perfume, in an ecstasy

28

of delight at being permitted to stop in such a
beautiful dwelling.
주거(지), 주택

"It certainly is a great joy to be alive," she
thought. "And there's no comparison between
(~와) 비교함
the dingy, crowded stories in which the bees live
우중충한, 거무칙칙한
and work and this house. The very quiet here is
조용한, 고요한
splendid."
정말 좋은[멋진], 훌륭한

Suddenly there was a loud sound of scolding
갑자기, 별안간   (소리가) 큰, 시끄러운   힐책, 꾸짖음
behind the walls. It was the beetle growling ex-
으르렁[딱딱]거리는
citedly in great anger. He seemed to be hustling
잔뜩 화가 나서   (거칠게) 떠밀다
and pushing someone along roughly, and Maya
밀어붙이다[젖히다], 밀치다   거칠게
caught the following, in a clear, piping voice full
(목소리가) 높은
of fright and mortification.
굴욕, 치욕, 억울

"Of course, because I'm alone, you dare to
혼자; 다른 사람 없이   감히 ~하다
lay hands on me. But wait and see what you
손을 대다
get when I bring my associates along. You are a
(사업, 직장의) 동료
ruffian. Very well, I am going. But remember, I
깡패, 악당   기억해라
called you a ruffian. You'll never forget *that*."
잊다, 잊어버리다

The stranger's emphatic tone, so sharp and
강한[단호한]   날카로운, 예리한
vicious, frightened Maya dreadfully. In a few
잔인한, 포악한, 악랄한   굉장히, 지독하게
moments she heard the sound of someone run-

ning out. The beetle returned and sullenly flung
down some nectar.

"An outrage," he said. "You can't escape those
vermin anywhere. They don't allow you a moment's peace."

Maya was so hungry she forgot to thank him
and took a mouthful of nectar and chewed,
while the beetle wiped the perspiration from his
forehead and slightly loosened his upper armor
so as to catch his breath.

"Who was that?" mumbled Maya, with her
mouth still full.

"Please empty your mouth—finish chewing
and swallowing your nectar. One can't understand a word you say."

Maya obeyed, but the excited owner of the
house gave her no time to repeat her question.

"It was an ant," he burst out angrily. "Do
those ants think we save and store up hour after hour only for them! The idea of going right
into the pantry without a how-do-you-do or a

30

by-your-leave! It makes me furious. If I didn't
허락을 청함   열 받게 하다, 분노하게 하다

realize that the ill-mannered creatures actually
깨닫다, 알아차리다, 인식[자각]하다   버르장머리 없는 생물

didn't know better, I wouldn't hesitate a second
(확신이 안 서서) 망설이다

to call them—thieves!"
thief(도둑, 절도범)의 복수

At this he suddenly remembered his own
갑자기

manners.

"I beg your pardon," he said, turning to Maya,
죄송합니다, 용서하십시오

"I forgot to introduce myself. My name is Peter,
소개하다

of the family of rose-beetles."
장미풍뎅이

"My name is Maya," said the little bee shyly.
수줍게

"I am delighted to make your acquaintance."
만나서 반갑습니다.(= Nice to meet you.)

She looked at Peter closely; he was bowing re-
열심히, 주의하여

peatedly, and spreading his feelers like two little
(접혀 있던 것을) 펼치다[펴다]   (곤충의) 더듬이[촉수]

brown fans. That pleased Maya immensely.
부채   엄청나게, 대단히

"You have the most fascinating feelers," she
대단히 흥미로운, 매력적인

said, "simply sweet...."

"Well, yes," observed Peter, flattered, "people
(의견을) 말하다   자기가 잘난 줄 착각하다

do think a lot of them. Would you like to see the

other side?"
뒤쪽, 반대쪽

"If I may."

The rose-beetle turned his fan-shaped feelers
to one side and let a ray of sunlight glide over
them.

"Great, don't you think?" he asked.

"I shouldn't have thought anything like them
possible," rejoined Maya. "My own feelers are
very plain."

"Well, yes," observed Peter, "to each his own.
By way of compensation you certainly have
beautiful eyes, and the color of your body, the
gold of your body, is not to be sneezed at."

Maya beamed. Peter was the first person to
tell her she had any good looks. Life was great.
She was happy as a lark, and helped herself to
some more nectar.

"An excellent quality of honey," she remarked.
"Take some more," said Peter, rather amazed
by his little guest's appetite. "Rose-juice of the
first vintage. One has to be careful and not spoil
one's stomach. There's some dew left, too, if
you're thirsty."

"Thank you so much," said Maya. "I'd like to fly now, if you will permit me."

The rose-beetle laughed.

"Flying, always flying," he said. "It's in the blood of you bees. I don't understand such a restless way of living. There's some advantage in staying in one place, too, don't you think?"

Peter courteously held the red curtain aside.

"I'll go as far as our observation petal with you," he said. "It makes an excellent place to fly from."

"Oh, thank you," said Maya, "I can fly from anywhere."

"That's where you have the advantage over me," replied Peter. "I have some difficulty in unfolding my lower wings."

He shook her hand and held the last curtain aside for her.

"Oh, the blue sky!" rejoiced Maya. "Good-by."

"So long," called Peter, remaining on the top petal to see Maya rise rapidly straight up to the

sky in the golden sunlight and the clear, pure air of the morning. With a sigh he returned, 한숨을 쉬면서 pensive, to his cool rose-dwelling, for though 깊은 생각[수심]에 잠긴, 수심 어린 it was still early he was feeling rather warm. 아직 이른 약간, 좀 He sang his morning song to himself, and it hummed in the red sheen of the petals and the 윤(기), 광택 radiance of the spring day that slowly mounted (따스하고 밝은) 빛[광휘] (서서히) 증가하다 and spread over the blossoming earth.
(더 넓은 범위로) 번지다[번지게 하다]

Gold and green are field and tree,

    Warm in summer's glow;
                (은은한) 불빛

All is bright and fair to see
      밝은, 눈부신, 빛나는
    While the roses blow.
  ~하는 동안   꽃이 피다, 꽃 피우다

What or why the world may be

    Who can guess or know?

All my world is glad and free
        기쁘고 자유로운
    While the roses blow.

Brief, they say, my time of glee;
           신이 남, 만족

    With the roses I go;

Yes, but life is good to me

    While the roses blow.

3

THE LAKE

"Dear me," thought Maya, after she had [이런, 아차] flown off, [날아가 버리다, 날아 흩어지다; 급히 떠나다] "oh, dear me, I forgot to ask Mr. Peter about human beings. [사람, 인간; (~s) [총칭적] 인간] A gentleman of his wide experience [경험] could certainly [분명히, 틀림없이] have told me about them. But perhaps I'll meet one myself to-[아마, 어쩌면] day."

Full of high spirits and in a happy mood of [진취적 기상; [pl.] 혈기 왕성; 기분 좋음] adventure, she let her bright eyes rove over the [모험] [두리번거리다] wide landscape that lay spread out below in all [광경, 풍경] [~아래] its summer splendor. [훌륭함, 장려(壯麗), 화려함]

She came to a large garden gleaming with a [빛나는, 환한] thousand colors. On her way she met many in-

sects, who sang out greetings, and wished her
a pleasant journey and a good harvest. — But
every time she met a bee, her heart went pit-a-
pat. After all she felt a little guilty to be idle, and
was afraid of coming upon acquaintances. Soon,
however, she saw that the bees paid not the
slightest attention to her.

Then all of a sudden the world seemed to turn
upside down. The heavens shone *below* her,
in endless depths. At first she was dreadfully
frightened; she thought she had flown too far
up and lost her way in the sky. But presently she
noticed that the trees were mirrored on the edge
of the terrestrial sky, and to her entrancement
she realized that she was looking at a great
serene basin of water which lay blue and clear in
the peaceful morning.

She let herself down close to the surface.
There was her image flying in reflection, the
lovely gold of her body shining at her from the
water, her bright wings glittering like clear glass.

And she observed that she held her little legs
…을 보다[(보고) 알다/목격하다] ; 관찰하다
properly against her body, as Cassandra had
제대로, 적절히
taught her to do.
teach의 과거, 과거분사: (방법 등을) 가르쳐[알려] 주다

"It's bliss to be flying over the surface of water
더없는 행복, 지복   수면, 표면
like this. It is, really," she thought.
                                    think의 과거, 과거분사

Big fish and little fish swam about in the clear
(물고기, 어류   swim의 과거
element, or seemed to float idly. Maya took good
(동물 본래의) 환경   (물 위나 공중에서) 떠[흘러]가다[떠돌다]
care not to go too close; she knew there was
조심하다, 주의하다
danger to bees from the race of fishes.
위험한   동류, 부류, 집단 ((의))

On the opposite shore she was attracted by
호수 건너에   마음을 끌다
the water-lilies and the rushes, the water-lilies
수련   골풀, 등심초
with their large round leaves lying outspread on
                                    활짝 펼쳐진
the water like green plates, and the rushes with
                        (둥그런) 접시, 그릇
their sun-warmed, reedy stalks.
                    갈대가 우거진 (식물의) 줄기[대]

She picked out a leaf well-concealed under
선택하다; 고르다   잘 감춰진
the tall blades of the rushes. It lay in almost to-
키 큰 풀잎들   거의 전체적으로
tal shade, except for two round spots like gold
그늘   ～만 제외하고   점
coins; the rushes swayed above in the full sun-
동전   (전후, 좌우로 천천히) 흔들리다[흔들다]
light.

"Glorious," said the little bee, "perfectly glori-
눈부시게 아름다운, 장엄한
ous."

She began to tidy herself. Putting both arms up behind her head she pulled it forward as if to tear it off, but was careful not to pull too hard, just enough to scrape away the dust; then, with her little hind legs, she stroked and dragged down her wing-sheaths, which sprang back in position looking beautifully bright and glossy.

Just as she had completed her toilet a small steely blue-bottle came and alighted on the leaf beside her. He looked at her in surprise.

"What are you doing here on my leaf?" he demanded.

Maya was startled.

"Is there any objection to a person's just resting here a moment or two?"

Maya remembered Cassandra's telling her that the nation of bees commanded great respect in the insect world. Now she was going to see if it was true; she was going to see if she, Maya, could compel respect. Nevertheless her heart beat a little faster because her tone had

been very loud and peremptory.
위압적인, 독단적인

But actually the blue-bottle was frightened.
사실, 실제로 / 깜짝 놀라다
When he saw that Maya wasn't going to let anyone lay down the law to her he backed down.
(주장을) 굽히다; 패배를 인정하다
With a surly buzz he swung himself on to a
성질 못된 윙윙 소리를 내면서
blade that curved above Maya's leaf, and said in
풀잎
a much politer tone, talking down to her out of
polite의 비교급
the sunshine:

"You ought to be working. As a bee you cer-
마땅히 ~해야 하다 / 벌답게
tainly ought. But if you want to rest, all right. I'll

wait here."
기다리다

"There are plenty of leaves," observed Maya.
많은 / (발언, 논평, 의견을) 말하다

"All rented," said the blue-bottle. "Now-a-
모두 임대되었다; 다 주인이 있다 / 요즘
days one is happy to be able to call a piece of
~할 수 있는(= can) / 한 조각의 땅
ground one's own. If my predecessor hadn't been
자기 소유의 / 전임자 / 잡아채지다, 잡아먹히다
snapped up by a frog two days ago, I should still
개구리 / 아직도, 여전히
be without a proper place to live in. It's not very
적절한, 제대로 된
pleasant to have to hunt up a different lodging
유쾌한, 즐거운 / 다른 임시 숙소를 찾아다니다
every night. Not everyone has such a well-or-
질서가 잡힌, 질서정연한
dered state as you bees. But permit me to intro-
~처럼 / 내 소개를 하겠다
duce myself. My name is Jack Christopher."

39

Maya was silent with terror, thinking how awful it must be to fall into the clutches of a frog.

"Are there many frogs in the lake?" she asked and drew to the very middle of the leaf so as not to be seen from the water.

The blue-bottle laughed.

"You are giving yourself unnecessary trouble," he jeered. "The frog can see you from below when the sun shines, because then the leaf is transparent. He sees you sitting on my leaf, perfectly."

Beset by the awful idea that maybe a big frog was squatting right under her leaf staring at her with his bulging hungry eyes, Maya was about to fly off when something dreadful happened, something for which she was totally unprepared.

In the confusion of the first moment she could not make out just exactly what *was* happening. She only heard a loud rustling like the

wind in dry leaves, then a singing whistle, a
(마른 잎을 스치는 / 휘파람을 부는 소리)
loud angry hunter's cry. And a fine, transparent
(성난 사냥꾼의 커다란 울부짖음 / 투명한)
shadow glided over her leaf. Now she saw—saw
(그늘 / ~위로 미끄러지듯 지나가다)
fully, and her heart stood still in terror. A great,
(완전히, 충분히 / 겁에 질려, 공포에 휩싸여)
glittering dragon-fly had caught hold of poor
(잠자리 / …을 잡다, …을 잡아채다)
Jack Christopher and held him tight in its large,
(꽉 붙잡다)
fangs, sharp as a knife. The blade of the rush
((동물의) 송곳니 / 갈대 잎)
bent low beneath their weight. Maya could see
(낮게 구부러지다[휘다])
them hovering above her and also mirrored in
(호버링. 공중 정지(공중에 정지해 있는 상태))
the clear water below. Jack's screams tore her
(비명 / 찢다)
heart. Without thinking, she cried:

"Let the blue-bottle go, at once, whoever you
(그쯤 해 둬라; ~을 놔줘라 / 곧, 즉시 / 누구든 …하는 사람(들))
are. You have no right to interfere with people's
(~을 침해하다, ~을 방해하다)
habits. You have no right to be so arbitrary."
(임의적인, 제멋대로인)
The dragon-fly released Jack from its fangs,
((잡고 있던 것을) 놓아 주다)
but still held him fast with its arms, and turned
(단단히 잡다)
its head toward Maya. She was fearfully fright-
(~쪽으로 / 굉장히, 지독하게)
ened by its large, grave eyes and vicious pin-
(근엄한, 위엄 있는 / 사나운, 공격적인 집게발)
cers, but the glittering of its body and wings
(반짝이는)
fascinated her. They flashed like glass and water
(매혹하다 / 비치다[번쩍이다]; 비추다)
and precious stones. The horrifying thing was
((액세서리, 미용) 보석 / 몸서리쳐지는, 소름끼치는)

41

its huge size. How could she have been so bold?

거대한   대담하게도[감히] …하다

She was all a-tremble.

온몸을 부들부들 떨다

"Why, what's the matter, child?" The dragon-

무슨 일이야?, 괜찮아?

fly's tone, surprisingly, was quite friendly.

놀랄 만큼: 의외로: 대단히   친절한, 우호적인

"Let him go," cried Maya, and tears came into

눈물이 쏟아지다

her eyes. "His name is Jack Christopher."

The dragon-fly smiled.

"Why, little one?" it said, putting on an inter-

흥미 있는 표정을 짓다

ested air, though most condescending.

거들먹거리는, 잘난 체하는

Maya stammered helplessly:

말을 더듬다   무력하게, 속수무책으로, 어찌할 수 없이

"Oh, he's such a nice, elegant gentleman, and

품격 있는, 우아한

he's never done you any harm so far as I know."

내가 알고 있는 바로는, 내가 아는 한

The dragon-fly regarded Jack Christopher

(어떤 감정, 태도를 갖고) …을 보다

contemplatively.

숙고하여 : 묵상에 잠겨서

"Yes, he is a dear little fellow," it replied ten-

부드럽게 대꾸하다

derly and—bit Jack's head off.

Maya thought she was losing her senses. For

정신을 잃다

a long time she couldn't utter a sound. In hor-

(소리, 말, 탄식 등을) 입 밖에 내다: 발언하다

ror she listened to the munching and crunching

아삭아삭[우적우적]하는 소리와 으드득 소리

above her as the body of Jack Christopher the

blue-bottle was being dismembered.

(죽은 동물을) 자르다

42

"Don't put on so," said the dragon-fly with its
mouth full, chewing. "Your sensitiveness doesn't
impress me. Are you bees any better? What
do you do? Evidently you are very young still
and haven't looked about in your own house.
When the massacre of the drones takes place
in the summer, the rest of the world is no less
shocked and horrified, and *I* think with greater
justification."

Maya asked:

"Have you finished up there?" She did not
dare to raise her eyes.

"One leg still left," replied the dragon-fly.

"Do please swallow it. Then I'll answer you,"
cried Maya, who knew that the drones in the
hive *had* to be killed off in the summer, and was
provoked by the dragon-fly's stupidity. "But
don't you dare to come a step closer. If you do
I'll use my sting on you."

Little Maya had really lost her temper. It was
the first time she had mentioned her sting and

43

the first time she felt glad that she possessed the

weapon.

The dragon-fly threw her a wicked glance. It had finished its meal and sat with its head slightly ducked, fixing Maya with its eyes and looking like a beast of prey about to pounce.

The little bee was quite calm now. Where she got her courage from she couldn't have told, but she was no longer afraid. She set up a very fine clear buzzing as she had once heard a sentinel do when a wasp came near the entrance of the hive.

The dragon-fly said slowly and threateningly:

"Dragon-flies live on the best terms with the nation of bees."

"Very sensible in them," flashed Maya.

"Do you mean to insinuate that I am afraid of you—I of you?"

With a jerk the dragon-fly let go of the rush, which sprang back into its former position, and flew off with a whirr and sparkle of its wings,

straight down to the surface of the water, where
it made a superb appearance reflected in the
mirror of the lake. You'd have thought there
were two dragon-flies. Both moved their crystal wings so swiftly and finely that it seemed as
though a brilliant sheen of silver were streaming
around them.

Maya quite forgot her grief over poor Jack
Christopher and all sense of her own danger.

"How lovely! How lovely!" she cried enthusi-
astically, clapping her hands.

"Do you mean me?" The dragon-fly spoke in
astonishment, but quickly added: "Yes, I must
admit I am fairly presentable. Yesterday I was
flying along the brook, and you should have
heard some human beings who were lying on
the bank rave over me."

"Human beings!" exclaimed Maya. "Oh my,
did you see human beings?"

"Of course," answered the dragon-fly. "But
you'll be very interested to know my name, I'm

sure. My name is Loveydear, of the order Odo-
잠자리목(目)
nata, of the family Libellulidae."
잠자리과

"Oh, do tell me about human beings," implored
~에 대해 말하다   애원하다, 간청하다
Maya, after she had introduced herself.
소개하다

The dragon-fly seemed won over. She seated
설득하다, 자기편으로 끌어들이다
herself on the leaf beside Maya. And the little
~옆에
bee let her, knowing Miss Loveydear would be

careful not to come too close.
조심하다, 주의하다
"Have human beings a sting?" she asked.
침

"Good gracious, what would they do with a
맙소사(= Oh my God)
sting! No, they have worse weapons against us,
더 나쁜, 더 심한(bad의 비교급)
and they are very dangerous. There isn't a soul
위험한
who isn't afraid of them, especially of the little
~을 두려워하지 않다   특히
ones whose two legs show—the boys."

"Do they try to catch you?" asked Maya,

breathless with excitement.
숨이 가쁜[찬]; 숨을 가쁘게 하는
"Yes, can't you understand why?" Miss Lovey-

dear glanced at her wings. "I have seldom met a
흘깃 쳐다보다   좀처럼[거의] …않는
human being who hasn't tried to catch me."

"But why?" asked Maya in a tremor.
(약간의) 떨림
"You see," said Miss Loveydear, with a modest
겸손한

46

smirk and a drooping, sidewise glance, "there's
히죽히죽[능글맞게] 웃다   곁눈으로 보다
something attractive about us dragon-flies.
멋진, 매력적인
That's the only reason I know. Some members
유일한 이유
of our family who let themselves be caught went
through the cruellest tortures and finally died."
잔혹한 고문   마침내, 결국
  "Were they eaten up?"
먹어치우다
  "No, no, not exactly that," said Miss Lovey-
틀림없이, 분명히
dear comfortingly. "So far as is known, man
격려[위안]가 되게: 안심하라는 듯
does not feed on dragon-flies. But sometimes he
~을 먹다[먹고 살다]   가끔, 때때로
has murderous desires, a lust for killing, which
사람을 죽이려 드는[죽일 것 같은] 욕구[욕망]
will probably never be explained. You may not
설명되다
believe it, but cases have actually occurred of
믿다, 신뢰하다   일어나다, 발생하다
the so—called boy—men catching dragon-flies
~라고 불리는
and pulling off their legs and wings for pure
~을 잡아뜯다   그저 재미로
pleasure. You doubt it, don't you?"
확신하지 못하다, 의심하다, 의문[의혹]을 갖다
  "Of course I doubt it," cried Maya indignantly.
분연히, 분개하여
  Miss Loveydear shrugged her glistening
(어깨를) 으쓱하다
shoulders. Her face looked old with knowledge.

  "Oh," she said after a pause, grieving and
잠깐 있다가   슬픔으로 창백해지다
pale, "if only one could speak of these things
openly. I had a brother who gave promise of a
터놓고, 드러내 놓고, 솔직하게

47

splendid future, only, I'm sorry to say, he was a
little reckless and dreadfully curious. A boy once
threw a net over him, a net fastened to a long
pole.— Who would dream of a thing like that?
Tell me. Would you?"

"No," said the little bee, "never. I should never
have thought of such a thing."

The dragon-fly looked at her.

"A black cord was tied round his waist between his wings, so that he could fly, but not fly
away, not escape. Each time my brother thought
he had got his liberty, he would be jerked back
horribly within the boy's reach."

Maya shook her head.

"You don't dare even think of it," she whispered.

"If a day passes when I don't think of it," said
the dragon-fly, "I am sure to dream of it. One
misfortune followed another. My brother soon
died."

Miss Loveydear heaved a deep sigh.

"What did he die of?" asked Maya, in genuine
진실한. 진심 어린
sympathy.
동정. 연민

Miss Loveydear could not reply at once. Great
즉시. 곧바로
tears welled up and rolled down her cheeks.
솟아나다   뺨으로 굴러 떨어지다

"He was stuck in a pocket," she sobbed. "No
주머니 속에 갇히다   흐느끼다
one can stand being stuck in a pocket."

"But what is a pocket?" Maya could hardly
거의 ~않다
take in so many new and awful things all at
끔찍한. 지독한
once.

"A pocket," Miss Loveydear explained, "is a
설명하다
store-room that men have in their outer hide.—
저장실. 창고   바깥 표면의[외부의] 가죽
And what else do you think was in the pocket
(이미 언급된 것에 덧붙여) 또[그 밖의] 다른
when my brother was stuck into it? Oh, the
~안에 갇히다
dreadful company in which my poor brother
끔찍한   동행
had to draw his last breath! You'll never guess!"
절대로 상상도 못할 것이다
"No," said Maya, all in a quiver, "no, I don't
떨림. 가벼운 전율
think I can.— Honey, perhaps?"
혹시. 어쩌면
"Not likely," observed Miss Loveydear with an
(의견을) 말하다
air of mingled importance and distress. "You'll
섞인   중요성   (정신적) 고통. 괴로움
seldom find honey in the pockets of human be-
좀처럼[거의] …않는
ings. I'll tell you.— A frog was in the pocket, and

a pen-knife, and a carrot. Well?"

펜나이프, 작은 주머니칼

"Horrible," whispered Maya.— "What *is* a

속삭이다, 작은 소리로 말하다

pen-knife?"

"A pen-knife, in a way, is a human being's

어느 정도는; 어떤 면에서는

sting, an artificial one. They are denied a sting

인공의, 인조의   거부되다, 허락되지 않다

by nature, so they try to imitate it.— The frog,

모방하다, 본뜨다

thank goodness, was nearing his end. One eye

고맙게도, 다행히   죽어가고 있었다.

was gone, one leg was broken, and his lower jaw

아래턱

was dislocated. Yet, for all that, the moment my

탈구되다   순간

brother was stuck in the pocket he hissed at him

쉬익[쉿] 하는 소리를 내다

out of his crooked mouth:

비뚤어진, 구부러진

"'As soon as I am well, I will swallow you.'

~하자마자   삼키다

"With his remaining eye he glared at my

남아 있는, 남은   ~을 노려[쏘아]보다

brother, and in the half-light of the prison you

감옥

can imagine what an effect the look he gave him

상상하다, 그리다   영향; 결과, 효과

must have had—fearful!— Then something even

무시무시한, 무서운

more horrible happened. The pocket was sud-

끔찍한, 지독한

denly shaken, my brother was pressed against

(무엇에) 바짝 대다[밀착시키다/밀착되다]

the dying frog and his wings stuck to its cold,

죽어가는   stick의 과거, 과거 분사

wet body. He went off in a faint.— Oh, the mis-

정신을 잃다, 실신하다   비참함

ery of it! There are no words to describe it."

말로는 표현할 수 없다

"How did you find all this out?" Maya was so horrified she could scarcely frame the question.

"I'll tell you," replied Miss Loveydear. "After a while the boy got hungry and dug into his pocket for the carrot. It was under my brother and the frog, and the boy threw them away first.— I heard my brother's cry for help, and found him lying beside the frog on the grass. I reached him only in time to hear the whole story before he breathed his last. He put his arms round my neck and kissed me farewell. Then he died—bravely and without complaining, like a little hero. When his crushed wings had given their last quiver, I laid an oak leaf over his body and went to look for a sprig of forget-me-nots to put upon his grave. 'Sleep well, my little brother,' I cried, and flew off in the quiet of the evening. I flew toward the two red suns, the one in the sky and the one in the lake. No one has ever felt as sad and solemn as I did then.— Have you ever had a sorrow in your life? Perhaps you'll tell me about it some other time."

"No," said Maya. "As a matter of fact, until now I have always been happy."

"You may thank your lucky stars," said Miss Loveydear with a note of disappointment in her voice.

Maya asked about the frog.

"Oh, *him*," said Miss Loveydear. "He, it is presumed, met with the end he deserved. The hard-heartedness of him, to frighten a dying person! When I found him on the grass beside my brother, he was trying to get away. But on account of his broken leg and one eye gone, all he could do was hop round in a circle and hop round in a circle. He looked too comical for words. 'The stork'll soon get ye,' I called to him as I flew away."

"Poor frog!" said little Maya.

"Poor frog! Poor frog indeed! That's going too far. Pitying a frog. The idea! To feel sorry for a frog is like clipping your own wings. You seem

52

to have no principles."
원칙, 원리

"Perhaps. But it's hard for me to see *any* one
…에게 어려운
suffer."
(질병, 고통, 슬픔, 결핍 등에) 시달리다; 고통받다

"Oh," Miss Loveydear comforted her. "that's
위로[위안]하다
because you're so young. You'll learn to bear
배우다   참다, 견디다
it in time. Cheerio, my dear.— But I must be
안녕, 잘 가
getting into the sunshine. It's pretty cold here.
꽤, 상당히, 매우
Good-by!"

A faint rustle and the gleam of a thousand
희미한 바스락 소리   (어디에 반사된) 어슴푸레한[흐릿한] 빛
colors, lovely pale colors like the glints in run-
옅은 색깔   반짝임
ning water and clear gems.
맑은 보석
Miss Loveydear swung through the green
swing 의 과거, 과거분사
rushes out over the surface of the water. Maya
수면 위로
heard her singing in the sunshine. She stood
and listened. It was a fine song, with something
귀 기울여 듣다
of the melancholy sweetness of a folksong, and
구슬픈, 울적한   민요
it filled the little bee's heart with mingled happi-
…으로 가득 차다   뒤섞인
ness and sadness.

Softly flows the lovely stream
부드럽게   개울, 시내
Touched by morning's rosy gleam
만지다, 건드리다, 닿다, 대다

Through the alders darted,
오리나무
Where the rushes bend and sway,
골풀, 등심초, 갈대   (좌우로 천천히) 흔들리다
Where the water-lilies say
수련
"We are golden-hearted!"

Warm the scent the west-wind brings,
향기, 향내
Bright the sun upon my wings,

Joy among the flowers!
기쁨   ~사이의
Though my life may not be long,
비록 ~일지라도
Golden summer, take my song!

Thanks for perfect hours!

"Listen!" a white butterfly called to its friend.
나비
"Listen to the song of the dragon-fly."

The light creatures rocked close to Maya, and
(전후, 좌우로 부드럽게) 흔들리다[흔들다]
rocked away again into the radiant blue day.
(따스하고 밝게) 빛나는
Then Maya also lifted her wings, buzzed fare-
들어올리다
well to the silvery lake, and flew inland.
은빛 호수   내륙으로, 뭍으로

54

4

EFFIE AND BOBBIE

When Maya awoke the next morning in the corolla of a blue canterbury bell, she
(꽃의) 화관[꽃부리]   초롱꽃
heard a fine, faint rustling in the air and felt her
희미한   바스락거리는 소리
blossom-bed quiver as from a tiny, furtive tap-
(유실수나 관목의) 꽃대[꽃받침]   아주 작은. 은밀한; 엉큼한
tapping. Through the open corolla came a damp
축축한
whiff of grass and earth, and the air was quite
(잠깐 동안) 훅 끼치는[풍기는] 냄새
chill.
추운. 쌀쌀한
   In some apprehension, she took a little pol-
우려. 불안, 걱정   꽃가루[화분]을 조금 먹다
len from the yellow stamens, scrupulously per-
(꽃의) 수술   양심적으로; 용의주도하게
formed her toilet, then, warily, picking her steps,
조심하여. 방심하지 않고
ventured to the outer edge of the drooping blos-
(위험을 무릅쓰고, 모험하듯) 가다   아래로 늘어진. 고개 숙인
som.

It was raining! A fine cool rain was coming down with a light plash, covering everything all round with millions of bright silver pearls, which clung to the leaves and flowers, rolled down the green paths of the blades of grass, and refreshed the brown soil.

What a change in the world! It was the first time in the child-bee's young life that she had seen rain. It filled her with wonder; it delighted her. Yet she was a little troubled. She remembered Cassandra's warning never to fly abroad in the rain. It must be difficult, she realized, to move your wings when the drops beat them down. And the cold really hurt, and she missed the quiet golden sunshine that gladdened the earth and made it a place free from all care.

A troop of migrating ants were passing by, and singing as they marched through the cool forest of grass. They seemed to be in a hurry. Their crisp morning song, in rhythm with their march, touched the little bee's heart with melancholy.

Few our days on earth shall be,
(수가) 많지 않은[적은]

Fast the moments flit;
휙 스치다[지나가다]

First-class robbers such as we
최고 (수준)의 강도[약탈자]

Do not care a bit!
조금도 개의치 않다; 눈도 깜짝하지 않다

They were extraordinarily well armed and
비상하게, 엄청나게, 유별나게, 이례적으로

looked saucy, bold and dangerous.
뻔뻔하고, 용감하고 위험한

The song died away under the leaves of the
사라져 가다, 희미해져 가다

coltsfoot. But some mischief seemed to have
(식물) 머위, 관동   (크게 심각하지 않은) 나쁜 짓[장난]

been done there. A rough, hoarse voice sounded,
거칠고 쉰 목소리

and the small leaves of a young dandelion were
민들레

energetically thrust aside. Maya saw a corpu-
정력적[활동적]으로; 효과적으로   뚱뚱한(fat을 피하기 위해 씀)

lent blue beetle push its way out. It looked like
딱정벌레

a half-sphere of dark metal, shimmering with
반구(半球)   어두운 금속성의   희미하게 빛나다

lights of blue and green and occasional black. It
가끔의

may have been two or even three times her size.

Its hard sheath looked as though nothing could
(칼집처럼 무엇을 보호하기 위한) 싸개[피복]

destroy it, and its deep voice positively fright-
파괴하다; 말살하다   (강조하여) 분명히

ened you.

"Make way, *I'm* coming. Make way."
길을 비켜라! (~이 지나가도록) 비켜 주다; (~에게) 자리를 내주다

He seemed to think that people should

step aside at the mere announcement of his approach.

The beetle moved with a clumsy lurch through the wet grass, presenting a not exactly elegant appearance. Directly under Maya's blossom was a withered leaf. Here he stopped, shoved the leaf aside, and made a step backward. Maya saw a hole in the ground.

"Well," she thought, all a-gog with curiosity, "the things there *are* in the world. I never thought of such a thing. Life's not long enough for all there is to see."

She kept very quiet. The only sound was the soft pelting of the rain. Then she heard the beetle calling down the hole:

"If you want to go hunting with me, you'll have to make up your mind to get right up. It's already bright daylight."

He was feeling so very superior for having waked up first that it was hard for him to be pleasant.

A few moments passed before the answer
지나가다
came. Then Maya heard a thin, chirping voice
작은 새나 곤충이 짹짹거리는
rise out of the hole.

"For goodness' sake, do close the door up
아이고, 세상에, 맙소사
there. It's raining in."
비가 들이치다
The beetle obeyed. He stood in an expectant
복종하다, 하라는 대로 하다   (신나는 일을) 기대하는
attitude, his head cocked a little to one side, and
태도   한 쪽으로 조금 삐딱하게 기울이다
squinted through the crack.
눈을 가늘게 뜨고[찡그리고] 보다
"Please hurry," he grumbled.
투덜대다, 툴툴거리다
Maya was tense with eagerness to see what
긴장한, 신경이 날카로운
sort of a creature would come out of the hole.
어떤 종류의 생물   구멍 밖으로 나오다
She crept so far out on the edge of the blossom
살금살금 움직이다, 살살 기다 (creep 의 과거, 과거분사)
that a drop of rain fell on her shoulder, and gave
빗방울   어깨   깜짝 놀라게 하다
her a start. She wiped herself dry.
닦아내다
Below her the withered leaf heaved; a brown
말라 죽은, 시든
insect crept out, slowly. Maya thought it was the
곤충   기어 나오다
queerest specimen she had ever seen. It had a
가장 기묘한, 정말 괴상한   표본
plump body, set on extremely thin, slow-mov-
통통한, 포동포동한, 토실토실한   극도로[극히] 가는
ing legs, and a fearfully thick head, with little
upright feelers. It looked flustered.
수직으로[똑바로] 선 더듬이   당황한, 허둥지둥하는

"Good morning, Effie dear."

The beetle went slim with politeness. He was all politeness, and his body seemed really slim.

"How did you sleep, my precious—my all?"

Effie took his hand rather stonily.

"It can't be, Bobbie," she said. "I can't go with you. We're creating too much talk."

Poor Bobbie looked quite alarmed.

"I don't understand," he stammered. "I don't understand.— Is our new-found happiness to be wrecked by such nonsense? Effie, think— think the thing over. What do *you* care *what* people say? You have your hole, you can creep into it whenever you like, and if you go down far enough, you won't hear a syllable."

Effie smiled a sad, superior smile.

"Bobbie, you don't understand. I have my own views in the matter.— Besides, there's some- thing else. You have been exceedingly indelicate. You took advantage of my ignorance. You let me think you were a rose-beetle and yesterday the

snail told me you are a tumble-bug. A consider-
able difference! He saw you engaged in—well,
doing something I don't care to mention. I'm
sure you will now admit that I must take back
my word."

Bobbie was stunned. When he recovered from
the shock he burst out angrily:

"No, I *don't* understand. I can't understand.
I want to be loved for myself, and not for my
business."

"If only it weren't dung," said Effie offishly,
"anything but dung, I shouldn't be so particu-
lar.— And please remember, I'm a young widow
who lost her husband only three days ago under
the most tragic circumstances—he was gobbled
up by the shrewmouse—and it isn't proper for
me to be gadding about. A young widow should
lead a life of complete retirement. So—good-by."

Pop into her hole went Effie, as though a puff
of wind had blown her away. Maya would never
have thought it possible that anyone could dive

into the ground as fast as that.

"People nowadays no longer appreciate fineness of character and respectability," Bobbie sighed. "Effie is heartless. I didn't dare admit it to myself, but she is, she's absolutely heartless. But even if she hasn't got the *right feelings*, she ought to have the *good sense* to be my wife."

Maya saw the tears come to his eyes, and her heart was seized with pity.

But the next instant Bobbie stirred. He wiped the tears away and crept cautiously behind a small mound of earth, which his friend had probably shoveled out of her dwelling. A little flesh-colored earthworm was coming along through the grass. It had the queerest way of propelling itself, by first making itself long and thin, then short and thick. Its cylinder of a body consisted of nothing but delicate rings that pushed and groped forward noiselessly.

Suddenly, startling Maya, Bobbie made one
깜짝 놀라게 하다
step out of his hiding-place, caught hold of the
숨어 있던 곳   ~를 잡다
worm, bit it in two, and began calmly to eat the
깨물어 두 토막을 내다
one half, heedless of its desperate wriggling or
(~에) 세심한 주의를 기울이지 않는   꿈틀거리는
the wriggling of the other half in the grass. It
was a tiny little worm.
아주 작은

At that moment she saw the half of the worm
바로 그 순간   ~의 반쪽
which Bobbie had set aside, making a hasty de-
황망히 출발하다
parture.

"Did you *ever* see the like!" she cried, sur-
무슨 이런 (…한) 일이(놀람 · 충격을 나타냄)
prised into such a loud tone that Bobbie looked
커다란, 시끄러운   주위를 둘러보다
around wondering where the sound had come
이상히 여기는; 이상한 듯한; 궁금한 듯
from.

"Make way!" he called.
길을 비켜라
"But I'm not in your way," said Maya.

"Where are you then? You must be somewhere."

"Up here. Up above you. In the bluebell."
(위치나 지위 면에서) …보다 위에[위로]
"I believe you, but I'm no grasshopper. I can't
믿다, 신뢰하다   메뚜기
turn my head up far enough to see you. Why did
…에 필요한 정도로, …할 만큼 (충분히)
you scream?"
(아픔, 무서움으로) 비명을 지르다; (흥분 등으로) 괴성을 지르다

"The half of the worm is running away."

"Yes," said Bobbie, looking after the retreating
fraction, "the creatures are very lively.— I've lost
my appetite."

With that he threw away the remnant which
he was still holding in his hand, and this worm
portion also retreated, in the other direction.

Maya was completely puzzled. But Bobbie
seemed to be familiar with this peculiarity of
worms.

"Don't suppose that I always eat worms," he
remarked. "You see, you don't find roses everywhere."

"Tell the little one at least which way its other
half ran," cried Maya in great excitement.

Bobbie shook his head gravely.

"Those whom fate has rent asunder, let no
man join together again," he observed.— "Who
are you?"

"Maya, of the nation of bees."

"I'm glad to hear it. I have nothing against the bees.— Why are you sitting about? Bees don't usually sit about. Have you been sitting there long?"

"I slept here."

"Indeed!" There was a note of suspicion in Bobbie's voice. "I hope you slept well, *very* well. Did you just wake up?"

"Yes," said Maya, who had shrewdly guessed that Bobbie would not like her having overheard his conversation with Effie, the cricket, and did not want to hurt his feelings again.

Bobbie ran hither and thither trying to look up and see Maya.

"Wait," he said. "If I raise myself on my hind legs and lean against that blade of grass I'll be able to see you, and you'll be able to look into my eyes. You want to, don't you?"

"Why, I do indeed. I'd like to very much."

Bobbie found a suitable prop, the stem of a buttercup. The flower tipped a little to one side so that Maya could see him perfectly as he raised himself on his hind legs and looked up at her. She thought he had a nice, dear, friendly face—but not so very young any more and cheeks rather too plump. He bowed, setting the buttercup a-rocking, and introduced himself:

"Bobbie, of the family of rose-beetles."

Maya had to laugh to herself. She knew very well he was not a rose-beetle; he was a dung-beetle. But she passed the matter over in silence, not caring to mortify him.

"Don't you mind the rain?" she asked.

"Oh, no. I'm accustomed to the rain—from the roses, you know. It's usually raining there."

Maya thought to herself:

"After all I must punish him a little for his brazen lies. He's so frightfully vain."

"Bobbie," she said with a sly smile, "what sort of a hole is that one there, under the leaf?"

Bobbie started.

"A hole? A hole, did you say? There are very

many holes round here. It's probably just an ordinary hole. You have no idea how many holes there are in the ground."

Bobbie had hardly uttered the last word when something dreadful happened. In his eagerness to appear indifferent he had lost his balance and toppled over. Maya heard a despairing shriek, and the next instant saw the beetle lying flat on his back in the grass, his arms and legs waving pitifully in the air.

"I'm done for," he wailed, "I'm done for. I can't get back on my feet again. I'll never be able to get back on my feet again. I'll die. I'll die in this position. Have you ever heard of a worse fate!"

"Wait," she cried, "I'll try to turn you over. If I try very hard I am bound to succeed. But Bobbie, *Bobbie*, dear man, don't yell like that. Listen to me. If I bend a blade of grass over and reach the tip of it to you, will you be able to use it and save yourself?"

Bobbie had no ears for her suggestion. Frightened out of his senses, he did nothing but kick and scream.

So little Maya, in spite of the rain, flew out of her cover over to a slim green blade of grass beside Bobbie, and clung to it near the tip. It bent under her weight and sank directly above Bobbie's wriggling limbs. Maya gave a little cry of delight.

"Catch hold of it," she called.

Bobbie felt something tickle his face and quickly grabbed at it, first with one hand, then with the other, and finally with his legs, which had splendid sharp claws, two each. Bit by bit he drew himself along the blade until he reached the base, where it was thicker and stronger, and he was able to turn himself over on it.

He heaved a tremendous sigh of relief.
"Good God!" he exclaimed. "That was awful. But for my presence of mind I should have fallen a victim to your talkativeness."

"Are you feeling better?" asked Maya.

Bobbie clutched his forehead.
(꽉) 움켜잡다

"Thanks, thanks. When this dizziness passes,
현기증, 아찔함

I'll tell you all about it."

But Maya never got the answer to her ques-
~에 대한 대답을 듣다

tion. A field-sparrow came hopping through
멧새과(科) 방울새의 일종   깡충깡충 뛰다

the grass in search of insects, and the little bee
…을 찾아서

pressed herself close to the ground and kept

very quiet until the bird had gone. When she
가버리다, 사라지다

looked around for Bobbie he had disappeared.
주위를 둘러보다   사라지다

So she too made off; for the rain had stopped
급히 떠나다

and the day was clear and warm.

5

THE ACROBAT

O h, what a day!

The dew had fallen early in the morning, and when the sun rose and cast its slanting beams across the forest of grass, there was such a sparkling and glistening and gleaming that you didn't know what to say or do for sheer ecstasy, it was so beautiful, so beautiful!

The moment Maya awoke, glad sounds greeted her from all round. Some came out of the trees, from the throats of the birds, the dreaded creatures who could yet produce such exquisite song; other happy calls came out of the air, from

flying insects, or out of the grass and the bushes,
곤충   관목, 덤불
from bugs and flies, big ones and little ones.
벌레, 작은 곤충 [곤충] 파리

Maya had made it very comfortable for her-
안락한, 편안한, 쾌적한
self in a hole in a tree. It was safe and dry, and
안전한
stayed warm the greater part of the night be-
따뜻한
cause the sun shone on the entrance all day
비추다   입구
long.

Once, early in the morning, she had heard a
woodpecker rat-a-tat-tatting on the bark of the
딱따구리   똑똑똑똑 두드리는   나무껍질
trunk, and had lost no time getting away. The
나무 기둥[몸통]
drumming of a woodpecker is as terrifying to a
(몹시) 무섭게[겁먹게] 하다
little insect in the bark of a tree as the breaking
open of our shutters by a burglar would be to us.
덧문, 셔터   절도범, 빈집털이범
But at night she was safe in her lofty nook. At
(인상적이게) 아주 높은[우뚝한] 곳[구석]에서
night no creatures came prying.
엿보다(peep), 탐색하다, 동정을 살피다
She had sealed up part of the entrance with
~을 봉하다   출입구
wax, leaving just space enough to slip in and
딱 ~만큼만 남기다
out; and in a cranny in the back of the hole,
(벽에 난 아주 작은) 구멍[틈]
where it was dark and cool, she had stored a
저장하다
little honey against rainy days.
~을 대비해서

This morning she swung herself out into the
sunshine with a cry of delight, all anticipation
as to what the fresh, lovely day might bring. She
sailed straight through the golden air, looking
like a brisk dot driven by the wind.

After a while Maya let herself down into a forest of grass, where all sorts of plants and flowers were growing. The highest were the white
tufts of yarrow and butterfly-weed—the flaming
milkweed that drew you like a magnet.

She took a sip of nectar from some clover and
was about to fly off again when she saw a perfect droll of a beast perched on a blade of grass
curving above her flower. She was thoroughly
scared—he was such a lean green monster—but
then her interest was tremendously aroused,
and she remained sitting still, as though rooted
to the spot, and stared straight at him.

At first glance you'd have thought he had
horns. Looking closer you saw it was his oddly
protuberant forehead that gave this impression.

72

Two long, long feelers fine as the finest thread
더듬이 최고로 가는[촘촘한] 실
grew out of his brows, and his body was the
이마
slimmest imaginable, and green all over, even
상상[생각]할 수 있는
to his eyes. He had dainty forelegs and thin,
앙증맞은 앞다리
inconspicuous wings that couldn't be very
이목을 끌지 못하는, 눈에 잘 안 띄는
practical, Maya thought. Oddest of all were his
현실적인, 실용적인 기묘하기 짝이 없는
great hindlegs, which stuck up over his body like
뒷다리
two jointed stilts. His sly, saucy expression was
대말, 죽마(竹馬) 교활하고 짓궂은 표정
contradicted by the look of astonishment in his
모순되다 깜짝[크게] 놀람
eyes, and you couldn't say there was any mean-
ness in his eyes either. No, rather a lot of good
오히려 꽤 많은
humor.

"Well, mademoiselle," he said to Maya, evi-
아가씨 (Miss에 해당)
dently annoyed by her surprised expression,
짜증이 난, 약이 오른
"never seen a grasshopper before? Or are you
메뚜기
laying eggs?"
알을 낳다
"The idea!" cried Maya in shocked accents. "It
충격을 받은 말투로
wouldn't occur to me. Even if I could, I wouldn't.
…에게 생각이 떠오르다
It would be usurping the sacred duties of our
(왕좌, 권좌 등을) 빼앗다[찬탈하다]
queen. I wouldn't do such a foolish thing."
어리석은, 바보같은

The grasshopper ducked his head and made such a funny face that Maya had to laugh out loud in spite of her chagrin.

"Mademoiselle," he began, then had to laugh himself, and said: "You're a case! You're a case!"

The fellow's behavior made Maya impatient.

"Why do you laugh?" she asked in a not altogether friendly tone. "You can't be serious expecting me to lay eggs, especially out here on the grass."

There was a snap. "Hoppety-hop," said the grasshopper, and was gone.

Maya was utterly non-plussed. Without the help of his wings he had swung himself up in the air in a tremendous curve. Foolhardiness bordering on madness, she thought.

But there he was again. From where, she couldn't tell, but there he was, beside her, on a leaf of her clover.

He looked her up and down, all round, before and behind.

"No," he said then, pertly, "you certainly can't lay eggs. You're not equipped for it. You haven't got a borer."

"What—borer?" Maya covered herself with her wings and turned so that the stranger could see nothing but her face.

"Borer, that's what I said.— Don't fall off your base, mademoiselle.— You're a wasp, aren't you?"

To be called a wasp! Nothing worse could happen to little Maya.

"I *never*!" she cried.

"Hoppety-hop," answered he, and was off again.

"The fellow makes me nervous," she thought, and decided to fly away. She couldn't remember ever having been so insulted in her life. What a disgrace to be mistaken for a wasp, one of those useless wasps, those tramps, those common thieves! It really was infuriating.

But there he was again!

"Mademoiselle," he called and turned round [돌아보다, 돌아서다]
part way, so that his long hindlegs [뒷다리] looked like [~처럼 보이다]
the hands of a clock [시계 바늘] standing at five minutes be- [6시 25분]
fore half-past seven, "mademoiselle, you must

excuse me [용서하다] for interrupting [방해하다(중단시키다/가로막다)] our conversation
now and then. But suddenly I'm seized [붙잡히다, 사로잡히다]. I must
hop. I can't help it [어쩔 수 없다], I must hop, no matter where.
Can't you hop, too?"

He smiled a smile that drew his mouth from [입이 양쪽 귀에 가 닿다]
ear to ear. Maya couldn't keep from laughing.

"Can you?" said the grasshopper, and nodded [고개를 끄덕이다]
encouragingly. [격려하여, 격려하듯이]
"Who *are* you?" asked Maya. "You're terribly [굉장히]
exciting." [들떠 있는, 안절부절못하는, 흥분한]
"Why, everybody knows who I am," said the
green oddity [이상한(특이한) 사람(것)], and grinned almost beyond the [(소리 없이) 활짝(크게) 웃다]
limits of his jaws.

"I'm a stranger in these parts [이곳에 온 지 얼마 안 되다]," she replied [대답하다]
pleasantly [상냥하게, 즐겁게], "else I'm sure I'd know you.— But [그렇지 않으면]
please note that I belong to the family of bees, [~에 속하다]
and am positively not a wasp." [(강조하여) 분명히]

76

"My goodness," said the grasshopper, "one and the same thing."

그게 그거다. 그거나 같은 것이다

Maya couldn't utter a sound, she was so excited.

"You're uneducated," she burst out at length.

무지한. 교양 없는. 배우지 못한   버럭 소리를 지르다

"Take a good look at a wasp once."

유심히 살펴보다. 자세히 들여다보다

"Why should I?" answered the green one.

내가 왜 그래야 하는데?

"What good would it do if I observed differences

다른 점. 차이

that exist only in people's imagination? You, a

존재하다   상상력. 상상

bee, fly round in the air, sting everything you

공중을 날아다니다   침을 쏘다

come across, and can't hop. Exactly the same

정확히, 분명히

with a wasp. So where's the difference? Hoppety-hop!"

And he was gone.

"But now I am going to fly away," thought Maya.

There he was again.

"Mademoiselle," he called, "there's going to be a hopping-match tomorrow. It will be held

높이뛰기 시합   열리다

in the Reverend Sinpeck's garden. Would you

목사

care to have a complimentary ticket and watch

무료 티켓. 초대권

the games? My old woman has two left over. She'll trade you one for a compliment. I expect to break the record."

기록을 깨다

"I'm not interested in hopping acrobatics," said Maya in some disgust. "A person who flies has *higher* interests."

관심[흥미]이 없다 곡예 혐오감, 역겨움, 넌더리

The grasshopper grinned a grin you could almost hear.

거의 웃음소리가 들리는 것 같은

"Don't think *too* highly of yourself, my dear young lady. Most creatures in this world can fly, but only a very, very few can hop. You don't understand other people's interests. You have no vision. Even human beings would like a high elegant hop. The other day I saw the Reverend Sinpeck hop a yard up into the air to impress a little snake that slid across his road. His contempt for anything that couldn't hop was so great that he threw away his pipe. And reverends, you know, cannot live without their pipes. I have known grasshoppers—members of my own family—who could hop to a height three

소수, 적은 수 관심, 흥미 시력, 눈; 시야 껑충 뛰어오르다 깊은 인상을 주다 뱀 ~가로질러 미끄러지듯 가다 경멸, 멸시 집어던지다 목사 메뚜기 300배

hundred times their length. *Now* you're impressed. You haven't a word to say. And you're inwardly regretting the remarks you made and the remarks you intended to make. Three hundred times their own length! Just imagine. Even the elephant, the largest animal in the world, can't hop as high as that. Well? You're not saying anything. Didn't I tell you you wouldn't have anything to say?"

"But how *can* I say anything if you don't give me a chance?"

"All right, then, talk," said the grasshopper pleasantly. "Hoppety-hop."

He was gone.

Maya had to laugh in spite of her irritation.

"Mademoiselle!" A blade of grass beside Maya was set swaying.

"Goodness gracious! Where do you keep coming from?"

"The surroundings."

"But do tell, do you hop out into the world just so, without knowing where you mean to land?"

"Of course. Why not? Can *you* read the future? No one can. Only the tree-toad, but he never tells."

"The things you know! Wonderful, simply wonderful!— Do you understand the language of human beings?"

"That's a difficult question to answer, mademoiselle, because it hasn't been proved as yet whether human beings have a language. Sometimes they utter sounds by which they seem to reach an understanding with each other—but such awful sounds! So unmelodious! Like nothing else in nature that I know of. However, there's one thing you must allow them: they do seem to try to make their voices pleasanter. Once I saw two boys take a blade of grass between their thumbs and blow on it. The result was a whistle which may be compared with the

chirping of a cricket, though far inferior in qual-
지저귐, 우짖음   (…보다) 못한[질 낮은/열등한]
ity of tone, far inferior. However, human beings
make an honest effort.— Is there anything else
         수고, 애: 노력   그밖에 또 무엇인가[다른]
you'd like to ask? I know a thing or two."

He grinned his almost-audible grin.
                소리가 들릴 것만 같은
But the next time he hopped off, Maya waited
                        깡총 뛰어 가버리다
for him in vain. She looked about in the grass
      허사가 되어[헛되이]
and the flowers; he was nowhere to be seen.

6

PUCK

Maya, drowsy with the noonday heat, flew leisurely past the glare on the bushes in the garden, into the cool, broad-leaved shelter of a great chestnut-tree.

On the trodden sward in the shade under the tree stood chairs and tables, evidently for an out-door meal. A short distance away gleamed the red-tiled roof of a peasant's cottage, with thin blue columns of smoke curling up from the chimneys.

Now at last, thought Maya, she was bound to see a human being. Had she not reached the very heart of his realm? The tree must be his property, and the curious wooden contrivances in the shade below must belong to his hive.

Something buzzed; a fly alighted on the leaf beside her. It ran up and down the green veining in little jerks. Maya watched its antics in the sunshine, then approached it and said politely:

"How do you do? Welcome to my leaf. You are a fly, are you not?"

"What else do you take me for?" said the little one. "My name is Puck. I am very busy. Do you want to drive me away?"

"Why, not at all. I am glad to make your acquaintance."

"I believe you," was all Puck said, and with that he tried to pull his head off.

"Mercy!" cried Maya.

"I must do this. You don't understand. It's something you know nothing about," Puck rejoined calmly, and slid his legs over his wings till they curved round the tip of his body.

"I'm more than a fly," he added with some
pride. "I'm a housefly. I flew out here for the
fresh air."

"How interesting!" exclaimed Maya gleefully.
"Then you must know all about human beings."

"As well as the pockets of my trousers," Puck
threw out disdainfully. "I sit on them every day.
Didn't you know *that*? I thought you bees were
so *clever*. You pretend to be at any rate."

"My name is Maya," said the little bee rather
shyly. Where the other insects got their self-
assurance, to say nothing of their insolence, she
couldn't understand.

"Thanks for the information. Whatever your
name, you're a simpleton. You've got to watch
out and be careful," he said. "That's the most
important thing of all."

But an angry wave of resentment was surging
in little Maya.

"I will teach you to be polite to a bee," she
cried.

Puck set up an awful howl.
울부짖다[법석을 떨다] (크고 시끄럽게)

"Don't sting me," he screamed. "It's the only
비명을 지르다

thing you can do, but it's killing. Please remove
죽이다   치우다

the back of your body. That's where your sting

is. And let me go, please let me go, if you pos-
놓아주다

sibly can. I'll do anything you say. Can't you

understand a joke, a mere joke? Everybody
유머, 농담   그저, 단순히

knows that you bees are the most respected of
존경하다

all insects, and the most powerful, and the most
힘센, 힘이 넘치는

numerous. Only don't kill me, please don't.
수가 많은

There won't be any bringing me back to life.

Good God! No one appreciates my humor!"
진가를 알아보다[인정하다]

"Very well," said Maya with a touch of

contempt in her heart, "I'll let you live on condi-
경멸, 멸시   조건부로

tion that you tell me everything you know about

human beings."

"Gladly," cried Puck. "I'd have told you any-
기꺼이; 기쁘게

how. But please let me go now."

Maya released him. She had stopped caring.
풀어 주다, 석방[해방]하다

Her respect for the fly and any confidence she
…에 대한 존중   신뢰

might have had in him were gone. Of what value

85

could the experiences of so low, so vulgar a creature be to serious-minded people? She would
have to find out about human beings for herself.

"Now tell me. What do you want to know
about human beings? I think I had best tell you
a few things from my own life. You see, I grew
up among human beings, so you'll hear just
what you want to know."

"You grew up among human beings?"

"Of course. It was in the corner of their
room that my mother laid the egg from which I
came. I made my first attempts to walk on their
window-shades, and I tested the strength of my
wings by flying from Schiller to Goethe."

"What are Schiller and Goethe?"

"Statues," explained Puck, very superior,
"statues of two men who seem to have distin-
guished themselves. They stand under the mirror, one on the right hand and one on the left
hand, and nobody pays any attention to them."

"What's a mirror? And why do the statues stand under the mirror?"

"A mirror is good for seeing your belly when you crawl on it. It's very amusing. When human beings go up to a mirror, they either put their hands up to their hair, or pull at their beards. When they are alone, they smile into the mirror, but if somebody else is in the room they look very serious. What the purpose of it is, I could never make out. Seems to be some useless game of theirs. I myself, when I was still a child, suffered a good deal from the mirror. I'd fly into it and of course be thrown back violently."

Maya plied Puck with more questions about the mirror, which he found very difficult to answer.

"Here," he said at last, "you've certainly flown over the smooth surface of water, haven't you? Well, a mirror is something like it, only hard and upright."

The little fly, seeing that Maya listened most respectfully and attentively to the tale of his experiences, became a good deal pleasanter in his manners. And as for Maya's opinion of Puck, although she didn't believe everything he told her, still she was sorry she had thought so slightingly of him earlier in their meeting.

"Often people are far more sensible than we take them to be at first," she told herself.

"I'd like to know how I could get into a human being's house."

"Fly in," said Puck sagaciously.

"But how, without running into danger?"

"Wait until a window is opened. But be sure to find the way out again. Once you're inside, if you can't find the window, the best thing to do is to fly toward the light. You'll always find plenty of windows in every house. You need only notice where the sun shines through. Are you going already?"

"Yes," replied Maya, holding out her hand. "I
have some things to attend to. Good-by. I hope
you quite recover from the effects of the ice
age."

And with her fine confident buzz that yet
sounded slightly anxious, little Maya raised her
gleaming wings and flew out into the sunshine
across to the flowery meadows to cull a little
nourishment.

Puck looked after her, and carefully meditated
what might still be said. Then he observed
thoughtfully:

"Well, now. Well, well.— Why not?"

7

IN THE TOILS

Maya flew in among the stems of the blackberry vines, which were putting forth green berries and yielding blossoms at the same time. As she mounted again to reach the jasmine, something strange to the touch suddenly laid itself across her forehead and shoulders, and just as quickly covered her wings.

It was the queerest sensation, as if her wings were crippled and she were suddenly restrained in her flight, and were falling, helplessly falling. A secret, wicked force seemed to be holding her feelers, her legs, her wings in invisible captivity.

(식물의) 줄기 · 덩굴 · 초록색 베리들이 달리다 · 꽃이 피어 있는 · 동시에 · ~으로 오르다 · 낯선 어떤 것 · 가로질러 놓이다 · 이마 · 덮다 · 정말 묘한 느낌, 가장 이상한 느낌 · 마치 ~인 것처럼 · 제대로 기능을 못 하게 만들다 · (물리력을 동원하여) 저지[제지] 당하다 · 어찌해 볼 수도 없이, 무력하게 · 은밀하고[비밀스럽고] 사악한 힘 · 더듬이 · 보이지 않는 올가미

But she did not fall. Though she could no
longer move her wings, she still hung in the air
rocking, caught by a marvelously yielding soft-
ness and delicacy, raised a little, lowered a little,
tossed here, tossed there, like a loose leaf in a
faint breeze.

Maya was troubled, but not as yet actually
terrified. Why should she be? There was no pain
nor real discomfort of any sort. Simply that it
was so peculiar, so very peculiar, and something
bad seemed to be lurking in the background.
She must get on. If she tried very hard, she
could, assuredly.

But now she saw a thread across her breast,
an elastic silvery thread finer than the finest
silk. She clutched at it quickly, in a cold wave of
terror. It clung to her hand; it wouldn't shake
off. And there ran another silver thread over her
shoulders. It drew itself across her wings and
tied them together—her wings were powerless.
And there, and there! Everywhere in the air and

above her body—those bright, glittering, gluey
반짝반짝 빛나는   끈끈한
threads!

Maya screamed with horror. Now she knew!
공포에 휩싸여
Oh—oh, now she knew! She was in a spider's
거미줄
web.

Her terrified shrieks rang out in the silent
겁에 질린 비명소리   크게 울리다[들리다]
dome of the summer day, where the sunshine
touched the green of the leaves into gold, and
닿다, 접촉하다
insects flitted to and fro, and birds swooped
(가볍게) 돌아다니다. 휙 스치다[지나가다]   급강하하다
gaily from tree to tree. Nearby, the jasmine sent
화사하게; 명랑하게   바로 가까이에
its perfume into the air—the jasmine she had
향기
wanted to reach. Now all was over.
끝나다

A small bluish butterfly, with brown dots
푸르스름한 나비   갈색 점이 있는
gleaming like copper on its wings, came flying
구리, 동
very close.

"Oh, you poor soul," it cried, hearing Maya's
가엾은 것, 불쌍한 것
screams and seeing her desperate plight. "May
비명, 고함   지독한 곤경, 절박한 역경
your death be an easy one, lovely child. I cannot
죽음   쉬운, 편안한
help you. Some day, perhaps this very night, I
아마, 어쩌면
shall meet with the same fate. But meanwhile
(나쁜) 운명, 숙명   그 동안에
life is still lovely for me. Good-by. Don't forget

the sunshine in the deep sleep of death."

And the blue butterfly rocked away, drugged by the sunshine and the flowers and its own joy of living.

The tears streamed from Maya's eyes; she lost her last shred of self-control. She tossed her captive body to and fro, and buzzed as loud as she could, and screamed for help—from whom she did not know. But the more she tossed the tighter she enmeshed herself in the web. Now, in her great agony, Cassandra's warnings went through her mind:

"Beware of the spider and its web. If we bees fall into the spider's power we suffer the most gruesome death. The spider is heartless and tricky, and once it has a person in its toils, it never lets him go."

At that moment she saw the spider herself- very near, under a blackberry leaf. At sight of the great monster, silent and serious, crouching there as if ready to pounce, Maya's horror was

indescribable. The wicked shining eyes were fas-
형언할[말로 다 할] 수 없는

tened on the little bee in sinister, cold-blooded
사악하게, 불길하게

patience.
인내력, 인내심

Maya gave one loud shriek. This was the
외마디 비명을 내지르다

worst agony of all. Death itself could look no
극도의 (육체적, 정신적) 고통

worse than that grey, hairy monster with her
털이 많은

mean fangs and the raised legs supporting her
송곳니   (넘어지지 않도록) 떠받치다

fat body like a scaffolding. She would come
비계(높은 곳에서 공사를 할 수 있도록 임시로 설치한 가설물)

rushing upon her, and then all would be over.
파도처럼 밀려오다

Now a dreadful fury of anger came upon
(격렬한) 분노, 격분

Maya, such as she had never felt before. For-
전에는 결코 느껴보지 못한, 이제껏 한 번도 느껴보지 못한

getting her great agony, intent only upon one
…에 열중하고 있는

thing—selling her life as dearly as possible—she
최대한 소중하게

uttered her clear, alarming battle-cry, which all
(입으로 어떤 소리를) 내다; (말을) 하다   (전쟁터에서의) 함성

beasts knew and dreaded.
몹시 무서워하는[두려워하는]

"You will pay for your cunning with death,"
대금을 지불하다; 빚을 갚다

she shouted at the spider. "Just come and try to
소리를 지르다, 고함치다

kill me, you'll find out what a bee can do."

The spider did not budge. She really was
약간 움직이다[움직이게 하다], 꼼짝하다

uncanny and must have terrified bigger crea-
이상한, 묘한

tures than little Maya.

Strong in her anger, Maya now made another
violent, desperate effort. Snap! One of the long
suspension threads above her broke. The web
was probably meant for flies and gnats, not for
such large insects as bees.

But Maya got herself only more entangled.
In one gliding motion the spider drew quite
close to Maya. She swung by her nimble legs
upon a single thread with her body hanging
straight downward.

"What right have you to break my net?" she
rasped at Maya. "What are you doing here?
Isn't the world big enough for you? Why do you
disturb a peaceful recluse?"

That was not what Maya had expected to
hear. Most certainly not.

"I didn't mean to," she cried, quivering with
glad hope. Ugly as the spider was, still she did
not seem to intend any harm. "I didn't see your
web and I got tangled in it. I'm so sorry. Please
pardon me."

The spider drew nearer.
더 가까이 다가오다

"You're a funny little body," she said, letting

go of the thread first with one leg, then with the
다리를 번갈아 가며

other. The delicate thread shook. How wonder-
연약한, 여린

ful that it could support the great creature.
지탱하다, 떠받치다

"Oh, do help me out of this," begged Maya, "I
빌다, 애원하다

should be so grateful."
고마워하는, 감사하는

"That's what I came here for," said the spider,
그러려고 왔다

and smiled strangely. For all her smiling she
이상하게, 묘하게   ⋯에도 불구하고(= in spite of⋯)

looked mean and deceitful. "Your tossing and
비열한; 성질이 나쁜, 심술궂은   기만적인, 부정직한

tugging spoils the whole web. Keep quiet one
망치다, 버려 놓다, 못쓰게 만들다

second, and I will set you free."
~을 자유롭게 풀어주다

"Oh, thanks! Ever so many thanks!" cried

Maya.

The spider was now right beside her. She
바로 옆에

examined the web carefully to see how securely
살펴보다, 조사하다   조심스럽게, 주의 깊게   단단히; 튼튼하게

Maya was entangled.
얽어매지다, (걸려서) 꼼짝 못하게 되다

"How about your sting?" she asked.
침

Ugh, how mean and horrid she looked! Maya
야비한, 비열한   진저리나는, 지독한

fairly shivered with disgust at the thought that
⋯로 (몸을) 떨다   혐오감, 역겨움, 넌더리

she was going to touch her, but replied as pleasantly as she could:

"Don't trouble about my sting. I will draw it
~에 대해서 걱정하지 마라   안으로 끌어당기다
in, and nobody can hurt himself on it then."

"I should hope not," said the spider. "Now,

then, look out! Keep quiet. Too bad for my web."
              (경고하는 말로) 조심해라
Maya remained still. Suddenly she felt herself
        가만히 있다
being whirled round and round on the same
빙그르르[빙빙] 돌다[돌리다]   제자리에서
spot, till she got dizzy and sick and had to close
                어지럽고 속이 울렁거리다
her eyes.— But what was that? She opened her

eyes quickly. Horrors! She was completely en-
재빨리   완벽하게 얽히다, 칭칭 감기다
meshed in a fresh sticky thread which the spider
          갓 뽑아낸 끈끈한 거미줄로
must have had with her.

"My God!" cried little Maya softly, in a quiv-
                                        떨리는 목소리로
ering voice. That was all she said. Now she saw

how tricky the spider had been; now she was re-
        영리하지만 사기꾼 같은 데가 있는, 교묘한
ally caught beyond release; now there was abso-

lutely no chance of escape. She could no longer
                    도망, 도피
move any part of her body. The end was near.

Her fury of anger was gone, there was only a
        (격렬한) 분노
great sadness in her heart.
        슬픔, 비탄

The spider dropped down to the ground, laid the end of the newly spun thread [새로 뽑은 거미줄] about a stone, and pulled it in tight [단단히 잡아당기다]. Then she ran up again, caught hold of the thread by which little enmeshed [매달려 있는, 얽혀 있는] Maya hung, and dragged her captive [포로] along.

"You're going into the shade [그늘로, 그늘진 곳으로], my dear," she said, "so that you shall not dry up [바싹 마르다, 바짝 말라붙다] out here in the sunshine. Besides [게다가, 더욱이], hanging here you're like a scarecrow [허수아비], you'll frighten away [~을 겁을 주어 (~에서) 쫓아내다] other nice little mortals [(영원히 살 수는 없는, 언젠가는 반드시 죽는) 생물들(여기서는 곤충들)] who don't watch where they're going. And sometimes the sparrows [참새] come and rob [털다, 도둑질하다] my web.— To let you know with whom you're dealing, my name is Thekla, of the family of cross-spiders [무당거미]. You needn't tell me your name. It makes no difference [차이가 없다, 문제가 아니다]. You're a fat bit, and you'll taste just as tender and juicy [부드럽고 육즙이 많은] by any name."

So little Maya hung [매달리다] in the shade [그늘] of the blackberry vine [블랙베리 덩굴], close [가까운] to the ground, completely at the mercy [자비] of the cruel [잔혹한, 잔인한] spider, who intended [의도[작정]하다] her to die by slow starvation [기아, 굶주림]. Hanging with her little [머리를 아래쪽으로 향해 거꾸로 매달리다]

head downward—a fearful position to be in—she soon felt she would not last many more minutes. She whimpered softly, and her cries for help grew feebler and feebler. Who was there to hear? Her folk at home knew nothing of this catastrophe, so *they* couldn't come hurrying to her rescue.

Suddenly down, in the grass, she heard some one growling:

"Make way! *I'm* coming."

Maya's agonized heart began to beat stormily. She recognized the voice of Bobbie, the dung-beetle.

"Bobbie," she called, as loud as she could, "Bobbie, dear Bobbie!"

"Who are you?" asked Bobbie. "So many people know me. You know they do, don't you?"

"I am Maya—Maya, the bee. Oh please, please help me!"

"Maya? Maya?— Ah, now I remember. You made my acquaintance several weeks ago.— The

deuce! You *are* in a bad way, if I must say so myself. You certainly do need my help. As I happen
확실히, 분명하게
to have a few moments' time, I won't refuse."
거절하다, 거부하다
"Oh, Bobbie, can you tear these threads?"

Bobbie crawled up on the leaf, caught hold of
~위로 기어오르다   ~을 (움켜)잡다
the thread by which Maya was hanging, clung to
~에 매달리다
it, then let go of the leaf. The thread broke, and
끊어지다
they both fell to the ground.
둘 다, 양쪽 모두
"That's only the beginning," said Bobbie.—
오직, 단지   시작
"But Maya, you're trembling. My dear child,
(몸을) 떨다, 떨리다
you poor little girl, how pale you are! Now who
창백한
would be so afraid of death? You must look
~을 두려워하다   죽음
death calmly in the face as I do. So. I'll unwrap
침착하게, 냉정하게   풀어주다
you now."

"Bobbie," Maya screamed, "the spider's com-
비명을 지르다
ing."

Bobbie went on unperturbed, merely laugh-
(마음이) 흔들리지[동요하지] 않는
ing to himself. He really was an extraordinarily
비상하게, 엄청나게
strong insect.
곤충
"She'll think twice before she comes nearer,"
재고하다, 숙고하다   더 가까이
he said.

But there! The vile voice rasped above them:

"Robbers! Help! I'm being robbed. You fat lump, what are you doing with my prey?"

"Don't excite yourself, madam," said Bobbie. "I have a right, haven't I, to talk to my friend. If you say another word to displease me, I'll tear your whole web to shreds. Well? Why so silent all of a sudden?"

"I am defeated," said the spider.

"That has nothing to do with the case," observed Bobbie. "Now you'd better be getting away from here."

Meanwhile Bobbie finished the unwrapping of Maya. He tore the network and released her legs and wings. The rest she could do herself. She preened herself happily. But she had to go slow, because she was still weak from fright.

"You must forget what you have been through," said Bobbie. "Then you'll stop trembling. Now see if you can fly. Try."

Maya lifted herself with a little buzz. Her wings worked splendidly, and to her intense joy she felt that no part of her body had been injured. She flew slowly up to the jasmine flowers, drank avidly of their abundant scented honey-juice, and returned to Bobbie, who had left the blackberry vines and was sitting in the grass.

"I thank you with my whole heart and soul," said Maya, deeply moved and happy in her regained freedom.

"Thanks are in place," observed Bobbie. "But that's the way I always am—always doing something for other people. Now fly away. I'd advise you to lay your head on your pillow early tonight. Have you far to go?"

"No," said Maya. "Only a short way. I live at the edge of the beech-woods. Good-by, Bobbie, I'll never forget you, never, never, so long as I live. Good-by."

8

THE BUG AND THE BUTTERFLY

Her adventure with the spider gave Maya something to think about. She made up her mind to be more cautious in the future, not to rush into things so recklessly. Cassandra's prudent warnings about the greatest dangers that threaten the bees, were enough to give one pause; and there were all sorts of other possibilities, and the world was such a big place—oh, there was a good deal to make a little bee stop and think.

It was in the evening particularly, when twilight fell and the little bee was all by herself, that one consideration after another stirred her mind. But the next morning, if the sun shone, she usually forgot half the things that had bothered her the night before, and allowed her eagerness for experiences to drive her out again into the gay whirl of life.

One day she met a very curious creature. It was angular and flat as a pancake, but had a rather neat design on its sheath; and whether its sheath were wings or what, you couldn't really tell. The odd little monster sat absolutely still on the shaded leaf of a raspberry bush, its eyes half closed, apparently sunk in meditation.

The scent of the raspberries spread around it deliciously. Maya wanted to find out what sort of an animal it was. She flew to the next-door leaf and said how-do-you-do. The stranger made no reply.

"How do you do, again?" And Maya gave its leaf a little tap.

The flat object peeled one eye open, turned it

한쪽 눈을 살짝 뜨다

on Maya, and said:

"A bee. The world is full of bees," and closed

~으로 가득차다

its eye again.

"I have plenty of honey," said Maya. "May I

많은

offer you some?"

주다, 제공하다

The stranger opened its one eye and regarded

(어떤 감정을 갖고) …을 보다

Maya contemplatively a moment or two. "What

숙고하여 : 묵상에 잠겨서

is it going to say this time?" Maya wondered.

궁금해하다

This time there was no answer at all. The one

전혀

eye merely closed again, and the stranger sat

그저, 오직

quite still, tight on the leaf, so that you couldn't

see its legs and you'd have thought it had been

다리

pressed down flat with a thumb.

납작하게 누르다   엄지손가락으로

"Whoever you are," cried Maya, "permit me to

누구든 간에   허용[허락]하다

inform you that insects are in the habit of greet-

알리다[통지하다]   ~하는 버릇이 있는

ing each other, especially when one of them

서로   특히

happens to be a bee."

The bug sat on without budging. It did not so

꼼짝도 하지 않고

much as open its one eye again.

105

"It's ill," thought Maya. "How horrid to be ill
on a lovely day like this. That's why it's staying
in the shade, too."

She flew over to the bug's leaf and sat down
beside it.

"Aren't you feeling well?" she asked, so very
friendly.

At this the funny creature began to move
away. "Move" is the only word to use, because
it didn't walk, or run, or fly, or hop. It went as if
shoved by an invisible hand.

"It hasn't any legs. That's why it's so cross,"
thought Maya.

When it reached the stem of the leaf it
stopped a second, moved on again, and, to her
astonishment, Maya saw that it had left behind
a little brown drop.

"How *very* singular," she thought—and
clapped her hand to her nose and held it tight
shut.

The veriest stench came from the little brown
[VERY의 최상급] 순전한, 더할 나위 없는 악취
drop. Maya almost fainted. She flew away as fast
거의 기절할 지경이다
as she could and seated herself on a raspberry,
where she held on to her nose and shivered with
(가볍게) (몸을) 떨다
disgust and excitement.

"Serves you right," someone above her called,
쌤통이다, 꼴 좋다, 고소하다, 그래 싸다
and laughed. "Why take up with a stink-bug?"
노린재(악취를 풍기는 벌레)

"Don't laugh!" cried Maya.

She looked up. A white butterfly had alighted
나비
overhead on a slender, swaying branch of the
가느다란   (천천히) 흔들리고 있는
raspberry bush, and was slowly opening and
closing its broad wings—slowly, softly, silen-
(폭이) 넓은 날개   천천히   부드럽게   조용히
tly, happy in the sunshine—black corners to its
검은 색 귀퉁이
wings, round black marks in the centre of each
동그란 검은 점   ~의 한가운데에
wing, four round black marks in all.

Ah, how beautiful, how beautiful! Maya forgot
her vexation. And she was glad, too, to talk to
성가심, 짜증
the butterfly. She had never made the acquain-
                              …와 사귀다, 아는 사이가 되다
tance of one before even though she had met a
great many.

"Oh," she said, "you probably are right to laugh. Was that a stink-bug?"

"It was," he replied, still smiling. "The sort of person to keep away from. You're probably very young still?"

"Well," observed Maya, "I shouldn't say I was—exactly. I've been through a great deal. But that was the first specimen of the kind I had ever come across. Can you imagine doing such a thing?"

"You see," he explained, "stink-bugs like to keep to themselves. They are not very popular, so they use the odoriferous drop to make people take notice of them. We'd probably soon forget the fact of their existence if it were not for the drop: it serves as a reminder. And they want to be remembered, no matter how."

"How lovely, how exquisitely lovely your wings are," said Maya. "So delicate and white. May I introduce myself? Maya, of the nation of bees."

The butterfly laid his wings together to look
날개를 접다
like only one wing standing straight up in the
똑바로, 일직선으로
air. He gave a slight bow.
가볍게 인사하다. 고개를 끄떡하다

"Fred," he said laconically.
간결하게; 말 수 적게
Maya couldn't gaze her fill.

"Fly a little," she asked.

"Shall I fly away?"
멀리 날아가 버리다
"Oh no. I just want to see your great white
그저, 단지
wings move in the blue air. But never mind. I
신경쓰지 마라
can wait till later. Where do you live?"
기다리다
"Nowhere specially. A settled home is too
특별히   가정에서 자리를 잡은
much of a nuisance. Life didn't get to be really
성가신[귀찮은] 사람[것/일], 골칫거리
delightful until I turned into a butterfly. Before
~이 되다[~으로 변하다]
that, while I was still a caterpillar, I couldn't
애벌레
leave the cabbage the livelong day, and all one
양배추
did was eat and squabble."
(하찮은 일로) 옥신각신하다[(티격태격) 다투다]
"Just what do you mean?" asked Maya,
mystified.
얼떨떨해진, 혼란스러워진
"I used to be a caterpillar," explained Fred.
애벌레   설명하다
"Never!" cried Maya.

"Now, now, now," said Fred, pointing both
feelers straight at Maya. "Everyone knows a butterfly is first a caterpillar. Even human beings
know it."

Maya was utterly perplexed. Could such a
thing be?

The butterfly perched beside the little bee on
the slender swaying branch of the raspberry
bush, and they rocked together in the morning
wind. He told her how he had begun life as a
caterpillar and then, one day, when he had shed
his last caterpillar skin, he came out a pupa or
chrysalis.

"At the end of a few weeks," he continued,
"I woke up out of my dark sleep and broke
through the wrappings or pupa-case. I can't tell
you, Maya, what a feeling comes over you when,
after a time like that, you suddenly see the sun
again. I felt as though I were melting in a warm
golden ocean, and I loved my life so that my
heart began to pound."

"I understand," said Maya, "I understand.
I felt the same way the first time I left our
humdrum city and flew out into the bright
scented world of blossoms."

The little bee was silent a while, thinking of
her first flight.— But then she wanted to know
how the butterfly's large wings could grow in the
small space of the pupa-case.

Fred explained.

"The wings are delicately folded together
like the petals of a flower in the bud. When the
weather is bright and warm, the flower must
open, it cannot help itself, and its petals unfold.
So with my wings, they were folded up, then
unfolded. No one can resist the sun when it
shines."

"No, no—one cannot—one cannot resist the
sunshine." Maya mused, watching the butterfly
as he perched in the golden light of the morning, pure white against the blue sky.

"Oh," said Fred, "I should like to fly now. The meadows on the hillside are full of yarrow and canterbury bells; everything's in bloom. I'd like to be there, you know."

This Maya understood, she understood it well, and they said good-by and flew away in different directions, the white butterfly rocking silently as if wafted by the gentle wind, little Maya with that uneasy zoom-zoom of the bees which we hear upon the flowers on fair days and which we always recall when we think of the summer.

9

THE LOST LEG

Near the hole where Maya had set herself up for the summer lived a family of bark-boring beetles. Fridolin, the father, was an earnest, industrious man who wanted many children and took immense pains to bring up a large family. He had done very well: he had fifty energetic sons to fill him with pride and high hopes. Each had dug his own meandering little tunnel in the bark of the pine-tree and all were getting on and were comfortably settled.

"My wife," Fridolin said to Maya, after they had known each other some time, "has arranged

things so that none of my sons interferes with
간섭하다. 개입하다. 참견하다
the others. They are not even acquainted; each
심지어 안면도 없다
goes his own way."

Once he came at an early hour, as he often
이른 시간에, 아침 일찍   종종, 자주
did, to wish her good-morning and ask if she
인사를 건네다
had slept well.

"Not flying to-day?" he inquired.
(…에게) 묻다

"No, it's too windy."
바람 부는
It was windy. The wind rushed and roared
돌진[맹진]하다   으르렁거리다
and flung the branches into a mad tumult. The
던지다, 팽개치다 (fling 의 과거, 과거분사)   소란, 소동
leaves looked ready to fly away. After each great
gust the sky would brighten, and in the pale
세찬 바람, 돌풍
light the trees seemed balder. The pine in which
더 벗겨지다   소나무
Maya and Fridolin lived shrieked with the voices
소리[비명]를 지르다
of the wind as in a fury of anger and excitement.
격렬한 분노   흥분
Fridolin sighed and said in a worried tone:
한숨 쉬다   걱정스러운 말투로
"Ah, life would be beautiful if there were no
woodpeckers."
딱따구리
Maya nodded.
고개를 끄덕이다
"Yes, indeed, you're right. The woodpecker
정말로, 사실
gobbles up every insect he sees."
게걸스럽게 먹어 치우다

114

"If it were only that," observed Fridolin, "if it were only that he got the careless people who fool around on the outside, on the bark, I'd say, 'Very well, a woodpecker must live too.' But it seems all wrong that the bird should follow us right into our corridors into the remotest corners of our homes."

"But he can't. He's too big, isn't he?"

Fridolin looked at Maya with an air of grave importance, lifting his brows and shaking his head two or three times. It seemed to please him that he knew something she didn't know.

"Too big? What difference does his size make? No, my dear, it's not his size we are afraid of; it's his tongue."

Maya made big eyes.

Fridolin told her about the woodpecker's tongue: that it was long and thin, and round as a worm, and barbed and sticky.

"He can stretch his tongue out ten times my length," cried the bark-beetle, flourishing his

115

arm. "You think: 'now—now he has reached the limit, he can't make it the tiniest bit longer.' But no, he goes on stretching and stretching it. He pokes it deep into all the cracks and crevices of the bark, on the chance that he'll find some-body sitting there. He even pushes it into our passageways—actually, into our corridors and chambers. Things stick to it, and that's the way he pulls us out of our homes."

"I am not a coward," said Maya, "I don't think I am, but what you say makes me creepy."

"See who's coming," cried Fridolin, "coming up the tree. Here's the fellow for you! I tell you, he's a—but you'll see."

Maya followed the direction of his gaze and saw a remarkable animal slowly climbing up the trunk. She wouldn't have believed such a crea-ture was possible if she had not seen it with her own eyes.

"Hadn't we better hide?" she asked, alarm getting the better of astonishment.

"Absurd," replied the bark-beetle, "just sit still and be polite to the gentleman. He is very learned, really, very scholarly, and what is more, kind and modest and, like most persons of his type, rather funny. See what he's doing now!"

"Probably thinking," observed Maya, who couldn't get over her astonishment.

"He's struggling against the wind," said Fridolin, and laughed. "I hope his legs don't get entangled."

"Are those long threads really his legs?" asked Maya, opening her eyes wide. "I've never seen the like."

Meanwhile the newcomer had drawn near, and Maya got a better view of him. He looked as though he were swinging in the air, his rotund little body hung so high on his monstrously long legs, which groped for a footing on all sides like a movable scaffolding of threads. He stepped along cautiously, feeling his way; the little brown sphere of his body rose and sank, rose and sank. His legs were so very long and thin that one alone would certainly not have been enough to support his body. He needed all at once, unquestionably. As they were jointed in the middle, they rose high in the air above him.

Maya clapped her hands together.

"Well!" she cried. "Did you ever? Would you have dreamed that such delicate legs, legs as fine as a hair, could be so nimble and useful—that one could really use them—and they'd know what to do? Fridolin, I think it's wonderful, simply wonderful."

"Ah, bah," said the bark-beetle. "Don't take things so seriously. Just laugh when you see something funny; that's all."

"But I don't feel like laughing. Often we laugh at something and later find out it was just because we haven't understood."

By this time the stranger had joined them and was looking down at Maya from the height of his pointed triangles of legs.

"Good-morning," he said, "a real wind-storm—a pretty strong draught, don't you think, or—no? You are of a different opinion?" He clung to the tree as hard as he could.

Fridolin turned to hide his laughing, but little Maya replied politely that she quite agreed with him and that was why she had not gone out flying. Then she introduced herself. The stranger squinted down at her through his legs.

"Maya, of the nation of bees," he repeated. "Delighted, really. I have heard a good deal about bees.— I myself belong to the general family of spiders, species daddy-long-legs, and my name is Hannibal."

The word spider has an evil sound in the ears of all smaller insects, and Maya could not quite conceal her fright, especially as she was reminded of her agony in Thekla's web.

Hannibal seemed to take no notice, so Maya decided, "Well if need be I'll fly away, and he can whistle for me; he has no wings and his web is somewhere else."

"I am thinking," said Hannibal, "thinking very hard.— If you will permit me, I will come a little closer. That big branch there makes a good shield against the wind."

"Why, certainly," said Maya, making room for him.

Fridolin said good-by and left. Maya stayed; she was eager to get at Hannibal's personality.

The wind had subsided some, and the sun shone through the branches. From below rose the song of a robin redbreast, filling the woods with joy. Maya could see it perched on a branch, could see its throat swell and pulse with the song as it held its little head raised up to the light.

"If only I could sing like that robin redbreast," she said, "I'd perch on a flower and keep it up the livelong day."

"You'd produce something lovely, you would, with your humming and buzzing."

"The bird looks so happy."

"You have great fancies," said the daddy-long-legs. "Supposing every animal were to wish he could do something that nature had not fitted him to do, the world would be all topsy-turvy. Supposing a robin redbreast thought he had to have a sting—a sting above everything else—or a goat wanted to fly about gathering honey. Supposing a frog were to come along and languish for my kind of legs."

Maya laughed.

"That isn't just what I mean. I mean, it seems lovely to be able to make all beings as happy as the bird does with his song.— But goodness gracious!" she exclaimed suddenly. "Mr. Hannibal, you have one leg too many."

Hannibal frowned and looked into space, vexed.

"Well, you've noticed it," he said glumly. "But as a matter of fact—one leg too few, not too many."

"Why? Do you usually have eight legs?"

"Permit me to explain. We spiders have eight legs. We need them all. Besides, eight is a more aristocratic number. One of my legs got lost. Too bad about it. However you manage, you make the best of it."

"It must be dreadfully disagreeable to lose a leg," Maya sympathized.

"I should say so," said Hannibal. "Now listen. We daddy-long-legs, you know, hunt by night. I was then living in a green garden-house. It was overgrown with ivy, and there were a number of broken window-panes, which made it very convenient for me to crawl in and out. The man came at dark. In one hand he carried his artificial sun, which he calls lamp, in the other hand a small bottle, under his arm some paper, and in his pocket another bottle. He put every-thing down on the table and began to think, because he wanted to write his thoughts on the paper.— You must certainly have come across paper in the woods or in the garden. The black on the paper is what man has excogitated—excogitated."

생각해 내다, 고안해 내다

"Marvelous!" cried Maya, all a-glow that she was to learn so much.

멋져! 굉장해! 놀라워!

"For this purpose," Hannibal continued," man needs both bottles. He inserts a stick into the one and drinks out of the other. The more he drinks, the better it goes. Of course it is about us insects that he writes, everything he knows about us, and he writes strenuously, but the result is not much to boast of, because up to now man has found out very little in regard to insects. He is absolutely ignorant of our soul-life and hasn't the least consideration for our feelings. You'll see."

목적   계속하다
필요하다   둘 다, 양쪽 모두   끼우다. 넣다   막대기
마시다   더 많이 마실수록
일이 잘 진행되다   물론, 당연히
곤충   쓰다. 적다
활기차게; 열심히
결과   별로 자랑할 것이 못되는
알아내다. 발견하다   ~과 관련하여[~에 대하여]
전적으로, 틀림없이   ~을 모르는, ~에 무지한
최소한의 고려

"Don't you think well of human beings?" asked Maya.

"Oh, yes, yes. But the loss of a leg"—the daddy-long-legs looked down slantwise—"is apt to embitter one, rather."

내려다보다   기울어져서[진], 비스듬히   ···하기 쉽다
나쁜 감정을 갖게 하다

123

"I see," said Maya.

"One evening I was sitting on a window-frame as usual, prepared for the chase, and the man was sitting at the table, his two bottles before him, trying to produce something. It annoyed me dreadfully that a whole swarm of little flies and gnats, upon which I depend for my subsistence, had settled upon the artificial sun and were staring into it in that crude, stupid, uneducated way of theirs."

"Well," observed Maya, "I think I'd look at a thing like that myself."

"Well, on that fateful night I saw from my position on the window-frame that some gnats were lying scattered on the table beside the lamp drawing their last breath. The man did not seem to notice or care about them, so I decided to go and take them myself. That's perfectly natural, isn't it?"

"Perfectly."

"And yet, it was my undoing. I crept up the leg of the table, very softly, on my guard, until I could peep over the edge. The man seemed dreadfully big. I watched him working. Then, slowly, very slowly, carefully lifting one leg at a time, I crossed over to the lamp. As long as I was covered by the bottle all went well, but I had scarcely turned the corner, when the man looked up and grabbed me. He lifted me by one of my legs, dangled me in front of his huge eyes, and said: 'See what's here, just see what's here.' And he grinned—the brute!—he grinned with his whole face, as though it were a laughing matter."

Hannibal sighed, and little Maya kept quite still. Her head was in a whirl.

"Have human beings such immense eyes?" she asked at last.

"Please think of *me* in the position *I* was in," cried Hannibal, vexed. "Try to imagine how I felt. Who'd like to be hanging by the leg in front of eyes twenty times as big as his own body and a mouth full of gleaming teeth, each fully twice as big as himself? Well, what do you think?"

"Awful! Perfectly awful!"

"Thank the Lord, my leg broke off. There's no telling what might have happened if my leg had not broken off. I fell to the table, and then I ran, I ran as fast as my remaining legs would take me, and hid behind the bottle. There I stood and hurled threats of violence at the man. They saved me, my threats did, the man was afraid to run after me. I saw him lay my leg on the white paper, and I watched how it wanted to escape- which it can't do without me."

"Was it still moving?" asked Maya, prickling at the thought.

"Yes. Our legs always do move when they're pulled out. My leg ran, but I not being there it didn't know where to run to, so it merely flopped about aimlessly on the same spot, and the man watched it, clutching at his nose and

126

smiling—smiling, the heartless wretch!—at my leg's sense of duty."

"I can't believe it without proof."

"Do you think I'll tear one of my legs off to satisfy you?" Hannibal's tone was ugly. "I see you're not a fit person to associate with. Nobody, I'd like you to know, *no*body has ever doubted my word before."

Maya was terribly put out. She couldn't understand what had upset the daddy-long-legs so, or what dreadful thing she had done.

"Really, someone ought to come and eat you up."

Hannibal had evidently mistaken Maya's good nature for weakness. For now something unusual happened to the little bee. Suddenly her depression passed and gave way, not to alarm or timidity, but to a calm courage. She straightened up, lifted her lovely, transparent wings, uttered her high clear buzz, and said with a gleam in her eyes:

127

"I am a bee, Mr. Hannibal."

"I beg your pardon," said he, and without saying good-by turned and ran down the tree-trunk as fast as a person can run who has seven legs.

Maya had to laugh, willy-nilly. From down below Hannibal began to scold.

"You're bad. You threaten helpless people, you threaten them with your sting when you know they're handicapped by a misfortune and can't get away fast. But your hour is coming, and when you're in a tight place you'll think of me and be sorry."

Hannibal disappeared under the leaves of the coltsfoot on the ground. His last words had not reached the little bee.

The wind had almost died away, and the day promised to be fine. White clouds sailed aloft in a deep, deep blue, looking happy and serene like good thoughts of the Lord. Maya was cheered. She thought of the rich shaded meadows by the woods and of the sunny slopes beyond the

lake. A blithe activity must have begun there by
this time. In her mind she saw the slim grasses
waving and the purple iris that grew in the rills
at the edge of the woods. From the flower of
an iris you could look across to the mysterious
night of the pine-forest and catch its cool breath
of melancholy. You knew that its forbidding
silence, which transformed the sunshine into a
reddish half-light of sleep, was the home of the
fairy tale.

    Maya was already flying. She had started off
instinctively, in answer to the call of the meadows and their gay carpeting of flowers. It was a
joy to be alive.

10

THE WONDERS OF THE NIGHT

Thus the days and weeks of her young life
이렇게 하여; 이와 같이 어린, 젊은
passed for little Maya among the insects
지나가다 ~사이에서
in a lovely summer world—a happy roving in
사랑스러운 여름 이동해 다니는, 방랑하는
garden and meadow, occasional risks and many
정원 목초지, 풀밭, 초원 가끔의 위험
joys. For all that, she often missed the compan-
기쁨, 즐거움 자주, 종종 그리워하다 동료, 친구
ions of her early childhood and now and again
유아기
suffered a pang of homesickness, an ache of
시달리다; 고통받다 갑작스러운 아픔, 고통 향수병(nostalgia)
longing for her people and the kingdom she had
…에 대한 갈망 왕국
left. There were hours, too, when she yearned
갈망하다, 동경하다
for regular, useful work and association with
규칙적인, 정기적인 유용한, 쓸모 있는 연계, 유대, 제휴
friends of her own kind.

However, at bottom she had a restless nature,
어째쓴

little Maya had, and was scarcely ready to settle down for good and live in the community of the bees; she wouldn't have felt comfortable.

Often among animals as well as human beings there are some who cannot conform to the ways of the others. Before we condemn them we must be careful and give them a chance to prove themselves. For it is not always laziness or stubbornness that makes them different. Far from it. At the back of their peculiar urge is a deep longing for something higher or better than what every-day life has to offer, and many a time young runaways have grown up into good, sensible, experienced men and women.

Little Maya was a pure, sensitive soul, and her attitude to the big, beautiful world came of a genuine eagerness for knowledge and a great delight in the glories of creation. Yet it is hard to be alone even when you are happy, and the more Maya went through, the greater became her yearning for companionship and love.

She was no longer so very young; she had grown into a strong, superb creature with sound, bright wings, a sharp, dangerous sting, and a highly developed sense of both the pleasures and the hazards of her life. Through her own experience she had gathered information and stored up wisdom, which she now often wished she could apply to something of real value.

There were days when she was ready to return to the hive and throw herself at the queen's feet and sue for pardon and honorable reinstatement. But a great, burning desire held her back—the desire to know human beings. She had heard so many contradictory things about them that she was confused rather than enlightened. Yet she had a feeling that in the whole of creation there were no beings more powerful or more intelligent or more sublime than they.

A few times in her wanderings she had seen people, but only from afar, from high up in the air—big and little people, black people, white people, red people, and such as dressed in many colors. She had never ventured close.

Once she had caught the glimmer of red near a brook, and thinking it was a bed of flowers had flown down. She found a human being fast asleep among the brookside blossoms. It had golden hair and a pink face and wore a red dress. It was dreadfully large, of course, but still it looked so good and sweet that Maya thrilled, and tears came to her eyes. She lost all sense of her whereabouts; she could do nothing but gaze and gaze upon the slumbering presence.

All the horrid things she had ever heard against man seemed utterly impossible. Lies they must have been—mean lies that she had been told against creatures as charming as this one asleep in the shade of the whispering birch-trees.

After a while a mosquito came and buzzed greetings.

133

"Look!" cried Maya, hot with excitement and
흥분과 기쁨에 들떠서
delight. "Look, just look at that human being
쳐다보다
there. How good, how beautiful! Doesn't it fill
you with enthusiasm?"
열광: 열정, 열의
The mosquito gave Maya a surprised stare,
놀랍다는 눈길로 보다
then turned slowly round to glance at the object
~로 눈을 돌리다   (욕망, 연구, 관심 등의) 대상
of her admiration.
감탄, 존경
"Yes, it *is* good. I just tasted it. I stung it.
맛보다   쏘다, 찌르다
Look, my body is shining red with its blood."
피
Maya had to press her hand to her heart, so
누르다, 바짝 대다
startled was she by the mosquito's daring.
깜짝 놀라다   대담성
"Will it die?" she cried. "Where did you
죽다   외치다
wound it? How could you? How could you screw
상처[부상]를 입히다   망치다
up your courage to sting it? And how vile! Why,
용기   극도로 불쾌한[나쁜]
you're a beast of prey!"
야수, 맹수
The mosquito tittered.
킥킥거리다
"Why, it's only a very little human being," it
answered in its high, thin voice. "It's the size
높고 가는 목소리로
called girl—the size at which the legs are covered half way up with a separate colored casing.
분리된, 따로 떨어진, 독립된
My sting, of course, goes through the casing but

134

usually doesn't reach the skin.— Your ignorance is really stupendous. Do you actually think that human beings are good? I haven't come across one who willingly let me take the tiniest drop of his blood."

"I don't know very much about human beings, I admit," said Maya humbly.

"But of all the insects you bees have most to do with human beings. That's a well-known fact."

"I left our kingdom," Maya confessed timidly. "I didn't like it. I wanted to learn about the outside world."

"Well, well, what do you think of that!" The mosquito drew a step nearer. "How do you like your free-lancing? I must say, I admire you for your independence. I for one would never consent to serve human beings."

"But they serve us too!" said Maya, who couldn't bear a slight to be put upon her people.

"Maybe.— To what nation do you belong?"

"I come of the nation in the castle park. The ruling queen is Helen VIII."

"Indeed," said the mosquito, and bowed low. "An enviable lineage. My deepest respects.— There was a revolution in your kingdom not so long ago, wasn't there? I heard it from the messengers of the rebel swarm. Am I right?"

"Yes," said Maya, proud and happy that her nation was so respected and renowned. Homesickness for her people awoke again, deep down in her heart, and she wished she could do something good and great for her queen and country.

Carried away on the wings of this dream, she forgot to ask about human beings. Or, like as not, she refrained from questions, feeling that the mosquito would not tell her things she would be glad to hear. The mite of a creature impressed her as a saucy Miss, and people of her kind usually had nothing good to say of others. Besides, she soon flew away.

Once, on a warm evening, having gone to
따뜻한
sleep earlier than usual, she woke up suddenly
평소보다 더 일찍   잠에서 깨다   갑자기
in the middle of the night—something that had
한밤중에
never happened to her before. When she opened
절대로 일어나지 않다
her eyes, her astonishment was indescribable:
(아주 커다란) 놀라움   형언할[말로 다 할] 수 없는
her little bedroom was all steeped in a quiet
잠겨[담겨져] 있다   조용한
bluish radiance. It came down through the en-
푸르스름한 (따스하고 밝은) 빛[광휘]   입구
trance, and the entrance itself shone as if hung
빛나다   마치 ~인 것처럼
with a silver-blue curtain.
은빛이 감도는 푸른색
Maya did not dare to budge at first, though
감히 ~하다   약간 움직이다[움직이게 하다], 꼼짝하다
not because she was frightened. No. Somehow,
겁먹게[놀라게] 만들다
along with the light came a rare, lovely peace-
드문, 보기 힘든, 희귀한
fulness, and outside her room the air was filled
~으로 가득 차다
with a sound finer, more harmonious than any
조화로운
music she had ever heard.
음악
After a time she rose timidly, awed by the
겁많게: 소극적으로
glamour and the strangeness of it all, and
화려함[매력]   이상함, 신기함, 낯섦
looked out. The whole world seemed to lie under the spell of an enchantment. Everything
마법에 걸린 상태
was sparkling and glittering in pure silver. The
반짝거리는   눈부신, 반짝이는   순수한   은
trunks of the birch-trees, the slumbering leaves
자작나무   잠든, 잠자는

were overlaid with silver. The grass, which from
her height seemed to lie under delicate veils,
was set with a thousand pale pearls. All things
near and far, the silent distances, were shrouded
in this soft, bluish sheen.

"This must be the night," Maya whispered
and folded her hands.

As she was about to fly off through the silver light to her favorite meadow, now lying full
under the moon, she saw a winged creature
alight on a beech-tree leaf not far away. Scarcely
alighted, it raised its head to the moon, lifted its
narrow wings, and drew the edge of one against
the other, for all the world as though it were
playing on a violin. And sure enough, the sound
came, the silvery chirp that filled the whole
moonlit world with melody.

"Exquisite," whispered Maya, "heavenly,
heavenly, heavenly."

She flew over to the leaf. The night was so
mild and warm that she did not notice it was

cooler than by day. When she touched the leaf,
cool의 비교급

the chirper broke off playing abruptly, and to
떠들썩하게 이야기하는 사람 / 갑자기(suddenly), 불쑥, 뜻밖에

Maya it seemed as if there had never been such
마치 —인 듯이

a stillness before, so profound was the hush that
고요, 정적 / 엄청난, 깊은; 완전한 / 침묵, 고요

followed. It was uncanny. Through the dark
뒤따르다 / 이상한, 묘한, 초자연적인

leaves filtered the light, white and cool.

"Good night," said Maya, politely, thinking
공손하게

"good night" was the greeting for the night like
인사

"good morning" for the morning. "Please excuse
용서하다

me for interrupting, but the music you make
방해, 중단

is so fascinating that I had to find out where it
대단히 흥미로운, 매력적인

came from."

The chirper stared at Maya, wide-eyed.
~을 응시하다 / 눈을 동그랗게 뜨고

"What sort of a crawling creature are you?" it
기어다니는

asked after some moments had passed. "I have
순간

never met one like you before."

"I am not a crawling insect. I am Maya, of the
곤충

nation of bees."

"Oh, of the nation of bees. Indeed, you live by
정말로, 실제로

day, don't you? I have heard of your race from the
~에 대해 듣다 / 종족

hedgehog. He told me that in the evening he eats
고슴도치

139

the dead bodies that are thrown out of your hive."

"Yes," said Maya, with a faint chill of apprehension, "that's so; Cassandra told me about him; she heard of him from the sentinels. He comes when twilight falls and snouts in the grass looking for dead bodies. But do you associate with the hedgehog? Why, he's an awful brute."

"I don't think so. We tree-crickets get along with him splendidly. We call him Uncle. Of course he always tries to catch us, but he never succeeds, so we have great fun teasing him. Everybody has to live, doesn't he? Just so he doesn't live off me, what do I care?"

Maya shook her head. She didn't agree. But not caring to insult the cricket by contradicting, she changed the subject.

"So you're a tree-cricket?"

"Yes, a snowy tree-cricket.— But I must play, so please don't keep me any longer. It's full moon, a wonderful night. I must play."

And the cricket set up its happy silvery strumming. Heard from close by, where Maya sat, the music was overpowering in its loudness.

The little bee sat quite still in the blue summer night listening and musing deeply about life and creation.

Silence fell. There was a faint whirr, and Maya saw the cricket fly out into the moonlight.

"The night makes one feel sad," she reflected.

Her flowery meadow drew her now. She flew off. At the edge of the brook stood the tall irises brokenly reflected in the running water. A glorious sight. The moonlight was whirled along in the braided current, the wavelets winked and whispered, the irises seemed to lean over asleep.

"Asleep from sheer delight," thought the little bee. She dropped down on a blue petal in the full light of the moon and could not take her eyes from the living waters of the brook, the quivering flash, the flashing come and go of countless sparks. On the bank opposite, the birch-trees glittered as if hung with the stars.

"Where is all that water flowing to?" she wondered. "The cricket is right. We know so little about the world."

Of a sudden a fine little voice rose in song from the flower of an iris close beside her, ringing like a pure, clear bell, different from any earthly sound that Maya knew. Her heart throbbed, she held her breath.

"Oh, what is going to happen? What am I going to see now?"

The iris swayed gently. One of the petals curved in at the edge, and Maya saw a tiny snow-white human hand holding on to the flower's rim with its wee little fingers. Then a small blond head arose, and then a delicate luminous body in white garments. A human being in miniature was coming up out of the iris.

Words cannot tell Maya's awe and rapture. She sat rigid.

The tiny being climbed to the edge of the blossom, lifted its arms up to the moonlight, and

looked out into the bright shining night with a
smile of bliss lighting up its face. Then a faint
더없는 행복, 지복   희미한, 가벼운
quiver shook its luminous body, and from its
떨림, 가벼운 전율   어둠에서 빛나는, 야광의; 빛을 발하는
shoulders two wings unfolded, whiter than the
어깨   날개   펼쳐지다
moonlight, pure as snow, rising above its blond
순수한
head and reaching down to its feet. How lovely it
발
was, how exquisitely lovely. Nothing that Maya
아주 아름답게, 절묘하게; 정교하게, 우아하게
had ever seen compared with it in loveliness.
…와 비교하다   사랑스러움, 어여쁨
   Standing there in the moonlight, holding its
hands up to heaven, the luminous little being
하늘을 향해 손을 쳐들다   어둠 속에서 빛나는, 야광의
lifted its voice again and sang. The song rang out
울려퍼지다
in the night, and Maya understood the words.
알아듣다, 이해하다

My home is Light. The crystal bowl
빛   크리스탈 볼[그릇]
Of Heaven's blue, I love it so!

Both Death and Life will change, I know,
둘 다, 양쪽 모두
But not my soul, my living soul.
영혼
My soul is that which breathes anew
영혼   호흡하다, 숨을 쉬다   다시, 새로
From all of loveliness and grace;
사랑스러움, 어여쁨   우아함
And as it flows from God's own face,

It flows from His creations, too.
창작품, 창조물

Maya burst into sobs. What it was that made

격렬히 흐느끼다, 울음을 터뜨리다

her so sad and yet so happy, she could not have

너무나 슬프고 너무나 행복한

told.

The little human being turned around.

돌아서다, 몸을 돌리다

"Who is crying?" he asked in his chiming

(소리내어) 울다   종이 울리는 것 같은 목소리로

voice.

"It's only me," stammered Maya. "Excuse me

말을 더듬다

for interrupting you."

방해하다, 중단시키다, 가로막다

"But why are you crying?"

"I don't know. Perhaps just because you are so

아마도, 어쩌면

beautiful. Who are you? Oh, do tell me, if I am

아름다운   제발 말해 주세요

not asking too much. You are an angel, aren't

무리한 것을 부탁[요구]하다; 호된 값을 부르다   천사

you? You must be."

"Oh, no," said the little creature, quite serious.

생물체   진지한, 심각한

"I am only a sprite, a flower-sprite.— But, dear

요정, 도깨비   꽃의 요정

little bee, what are you doing out here in the

meadow so late at night?"

The sprite flew over to a curving iris blade

날아서 건너오다   곡선을 이룬, 휘어진   (한 가닥의) 풀잎

beside Maya and regarded her long and kindly

(어떤 감정, 태도를 갖고) …을 보다

from his swaying perch in the moonlight.

(천천히) 흔들리는 높은 자리

Maya told him all about herself, what she had
done, what she knew, and what she longed for.
And while she spoke, his eyes never left her,
those large dark eyes glowing in the white fairy
face under the golden hair that ever and anon
shone like silver in the moonlight.

When she finished he stroked her head and
looked at her so warmly and lovingly that the
little bee, beside herself with joy, had to lower
her gaze.

"We sprites," he explained, "live seven nights,
but we must stay in the flower in which we are
born, else we die at dawn."

Maya opened her eyes wide in terror.

"Then hurry, hurry! Fly back into your flower!"

The, sprite shook his head sadly.

"Too late.— But listen. I have more to tell you.
Most of us sprites are glad to leave our flowers
never to return, because a great happiness is
connected with our leaving. We are endowed
with a remarkable power: before we die, we can

145

fulfill the dearest wish of the first creature we meet. It is when we make up our minds seriously to leave the flower for the purpose of making someone happy that our wings grow."

"How wonderful!" cried Maya. "I'd leave the flower too, then. It must be lovely to fulfill another person's wish."

That *she* was the first being whom the sprite on his flight from the flower had met, did not occur to her.

"And then—must you die?"

The sprite nodded, but not sadly this time.

"We live to see the dawn still," he said, "but when the dew falls, we are drawn into the fine cobwebby veils that float above the grass and the flowers of the meadows. Haven't you often noticed that the veils shine white as though a light were inside them? It's the sprites, their wings and their garments. When the light rises we change into dew-drops. The plants drink us and we become a part of their growing and

blooming until in time we rise again as sprites
from out their flowers."

"Then you were once another sprite?" asked
Maya, tense, breathless with interest.
The earnest eyes said yes.
"But I have forgotten my earlier existence. We
forget everything in our flower-sleep."

"Oh, what a lovely fate!"
"It is the same as that of all earthly creatures,
when you really come to think of it, even if it
isn't always flowers out of which they wake up
from their sleep of death. But we won't talk of
that to-night."

"Oh, I'm so happy!" cried Maya.

"Then you haven't got a wish? You're the first
person I've met, you know, and I possess the
power to grant your dearest wish."
"I? But I'm only a bee. No, it's too much. It
would be too great a joy. I don't deserve it, I
don't deserve that you should be so good to me."
"No one deserves the good and the beautiful.

The good and the beautiful come to us like the sunshine."

Maya's heart beat stormily. Oh, she did have a wish, a burning wish, but she didn't dare confess it.

The elf seemed to guess; he smiled so you couldn't keep anything a secret from him.

"Well?" He stroked his golden hair off his pure forehead.

"I'd like to know human beings at their best and most beautiful," said the little bee.

She spoke quickly and hotly. She was afraid she would be told that so great a wish could not be granted.

But the sprite drew himself up, his expression was serious and serene, his eyes shone with confidence. He took Maya's trembling hand and said:

"Come. We'll fly together. Your wish shall be granted."

WITH THE SPRITE

And so Maya and the flower-sprite started
off together in the bright mid-summer
night, flying low over the blossomy meadow.
His white reflection crossing the brook shone as
though a star were gliding through the water.

As they were passing between a double row
of high poplar-trees, something whirred above
them; a dark moth, as big and strong as a bird,
crossed their way.

"One moment, wait one moment, please," the
sprite called.

Maya was surprised to see how readily the
moth responded.

All three alighted on a high poplar branch, from which there was a far view out upon the tranquil, moonlit landscape.

"Who is your companion?" the moth asked the sprite.

"A bee. I met her just as I was leaving my flower."

The moth seemed to realize what that meant. He looked at Maya almost enviously.

"You fortunate creature!" he said in a low, serious, musing tone, shaking his head to and fro.

"Is the bat still abroad, or has he gone to rest?"

This was the question for which the sprite had stopped the moth.

"Oh, he's gone to rest long ago. You want to know, do you, on account of your companion?"

The sprite nodded. Maya was dying to find

out what a bat was, but the sprite seemed to be in a hurry. With a charming gesture of restlessness he tossed his shining hair back from his forehead.

"Come, Maya," he said, "we must hurry. The night is so short."

"Shall I carry you part of the way?" asked the moth.

The sprite thanked him but declined. "Some other time!" he called.

"Then it will be never," thought Maya as they flew away, "because at dawn the flower-sprite must die."

Maya and the flower-sprite flew through the dense shrubbery of a garden. The glory of it in the dimmed moonlight was beyond the power of mortal lips to say. An intoxicatingly sweet cool breath of dew and slumbering flowers transformed all things into unutterable blessings. The lilac grapes of the acacias sparkled in freshness, the June rose-tree looked like a small blooming heaven hung with red lamps, the white stars of the jasmine glowed palely, sadly, and poured out their perfume as if, in this one hour, to make a gift of their all.

Maya was dazed. She pressed the sprite's hand and looked at him. A light of bliss shone from his eyes.

"Who could have dreamed of this!" whispered the little bee.

Just then she saw something that sent a pang through her.

"Oh," she cried, "look! A star has fallen! It's straying about and can't find its way back to its place in the sky."

"That's a firefly," said the flower-sprite, with- out a smile.

Now, in the midst of her amazement, Maya realized for the first time why the sprite seemed so dear and kind. He never laughed at her igno- rance; on the contrary, he helped her when she went wrong.

"They are odd little creatures," the sprite continued. "They carry their own light about with them on warm summer nights and enliven the dark under the shrubbery where the moonlight doesn't shine through. So firefly can keep tryst with firefly even in the dark. Later, when we come to the human beings, you will make the acquaintance of one of them."

"Why?" asked Maya.

"You'll soon see."

By this time they had reached an arbor completely overgrown with jasmine and woodbine. They descended almost to the ground. From close by, within the arbor, came the sound of faint whispering. The flower-sprite beckoned to a firefly.

"Would you be good enough," he asked, "to give us a little light? We have to push through these dark leaves here; we want to get to the inside of the jasmine-arbor."

"But your glow is much brighter than mine."

"I think so, too," put in Maya, more to hide
(남이 말하는 데) 끼어들다[거들다]
her excitement than anything else.
흥분, 신남   무슨 다른 것
"I must wrap myself up in a leaf," explained
(보호 등을 하기 위해) 싸다[둘러싸다]   설명하다
the sprite, "else the human beings would see me
and be frightened. We sprites appear to human
놀라게 하다   나타나다
beings only in their dreams."

"I see," said the firefly. "I am at your service. I
뭐든지 말만 해. 마음대로 부려도 돼
will do what I can.— Won't the great beast with
짐승
you hurt me?"
해를 입히다, 상처를 주다
The sprite shook his head no, and the firefly
아니라고 고개를 흔들다
believed him.
믿다, 신뢰하다
The sprite now took a leaf and wrapped
감싸다
himself in it; the gleam of his white garments
was completely hidden. Then he picked a little
꺾다, 집다
bluebell from the grass and put it on his shin-
블루벨(초롱꽃)   빛나는 머리에 쓰다
ing head like a helmet. The only bit of him left
헬멧처럼
exposed was his face, which was so small that
노출된, 드러난
surely no one would notice it. He asked the firefly to perch on his shoulder and with its wing to
걸터 앉다
dim its lamp on the one side so as to keep the
dazzle out of his eyes.
눈부심

"Come now," he said, taking Maya's hand. "We had better climb up right here."

The little bee was thinking of something the sprite had said, and as they clambered up the vine, she asked:

"Do human beings dream when they sleep?"

"Not only then. They dream sometimes even when they are awake. They sit with their bodies a little limp, their heads bent a little forward, and their eyes searching the distance, as if to see into the very heavens. Their dreams are always lovelier than life. That's why we appear to them in their dreams."

The sprite now laid his tiny finger on his lips, bent aside a small blooming sprig of jasmine, and gently pushed Maya ahead.

"Look down," he said softly, "you'll see what you have been wishing to see."

The little bee looked and saw two human beings sitting on a bench in the shadows cast by the moonlight—a boy and a girl, the girl with her

155

head leaning on the boy's shoulder, and the boy
holding his arm around the girl as if to protect
her. They sat in complete stillness, looking wide-
eyed into the night. It was as quiet as if they had
both gone to sleep. Only from a distance came
the chirping of the crickets, and slowly, slowly
the moonlight drifted through the leaves.

Maya, transported out of herself, gazed into
the girl's face. Although it looked pale and
wistful, it seemed to be transfused by the hidden
radiance of a great happiness. Above her large
eyes lay golden hair, like the golden hair of the
sprite, and upon it rested the heavenly sheen
of the midsummer night. From her red lips,
slightly parted, came a breath of rapture and
melancholy, as if she wanted to offer everything
that was hers to the man by her side for his happiness.

And now she turned to him, pulled his head
down, and whispered a magical something
that brought a smile to his face such as Maya

thought no earthly being could wear. In his eyes
세속적인 존재, 이 세상에 살고 있는 존재
gleamed a happiness and a vigor as if the whole
big world were his to own, and suffering and
고통, 괴로움
misfortune were banished forever from the face
불운, 불행   사라지게 만들다; 제거하다
of the earth.

Maya somehow had no desire to know what
알고 싶지 않다
he said to the girl in reply. Her heart quivered as
대답, 응답   (가볍게) 떨다[떨리다]
though the ecstasy that emanated from the two
황홀감; 황홀경   발하다, 내뿜다
human beings was also hers.

"Now I have seen the most glorious thing that
눈부시게 아름다운, 장엄한
my eyes will ever behold," she whispered to her-
바라보다
self. "I know now that human beings are most
beautiful when they are in love."
사랑에 빠져 있다
How long Maya stayed behind the leaves
~의 뒤에
without stirring, lost in looking at the boy and
꼼짝도 하지 않고, 숨 죽이고
girl, she did not know. When she turned round,
돌아보다
the firefly's lamp had been extinguished, the
(불을) 끄다
sprite was gone. Through the doorway of the
사라지다   출입구
arbor far across the country on the distant
정자   (거리가) 먼
horizon showed a narrow streak of red.
수평선, 지평선   가는, 좁은   기다란 줄 모양의 것

12

ALOIS, LADYBIRD AND POET

The sun was risen high above the tops of
높이 떠 있다
the beech-trees when Maya awoke in her
너도밤나무   잠에서 깨다 (AWAKE의 과거)
woodland retreat. In the first moments, the
숲속에 있는 조용한 곳
moonlight, the chirping of the cricket, the mid-
달빛   귀뚜라미 울음소리
summer night meadow, the lovely sprite, the
                목초지, 초원, 풀밭   요정, 도깨비
boy and the girl in the arbor, all seemed the per-
                        (나뭇가지나 덩굴로 덮인) 정자
ishing fancies of a delicious dream.
            달콤한 꿈, 아름다운 꿈
    Yet here it was almost midday; and she
                            거의
remembered slipping back into her chamber
기억해내다   침실, 방
in the chill of dawn. So it had all been real, she
        냉기, 한기   진짜의, 실제의
had spent the night with the flower-sprite and
                                꽃의 요정
had seen the two human beings, with their arms

round each other, in the arbor of woodbine and
인동덩굴, 양담쟁이(Virginia creeper)
jasmine.

The sun outside was glowing hot on the
뜨겁게 타오르다
leaves, a warm wind was stirring, and Maya
따뜻한 바람   젓다. 약간 흔들다
heard the mixed chorus of thousands of insects.
섞인, 혼합된   합창. 이구동성   곤충
Ah, what these knew, and what *she* knew! So
proud was she of the great thing that had hap-
자랑스러운   대단한, 위대한   우연히 일어나다
pened to her that she couldn't get out to the others fast enough; she thought they must read it in
빠른, 신속한   충분히   모습만 보고도 알다
her very looks.

But in the sunlight everything was the same
as ever. Nothing was changed; nothing recalled
여전히[변함이 없이] …로   변하다   생각나게 하다
the blue moonlit night. The insects came, said
푸른 달빛이 비치는
how-do-you-do, and left; yonder, the meadow
안녕하세요. 인사하다   저기 있는[보이는]
was a scene of bustling activity; the insects,
부산한, 북적거리는
birds and butterflies hopped, flew and flitted in
돌아다니다. 휙 스치다
the hot flickering air around the tall, gay mid-
깜박거리는. 아른거리는   (색채가) 화려한[화사한]
summer flowers.

Sadness fell upon Maya. There was no one
슬픔   ~에(게) 덤벼[달려]들다
in the world to share her joys and sorrows. She
나누다. 공유하다 기쁨, 행복   슬픔, 비탄
couldn't make up her mind to fly over and join

the others in the meadow. No, she would go to the woods. The woods were serious and solemn. They suited her mood.

How many mysteries and marvels lie hidden in the dim depths of the woods, no one suspects who hurries unobservant along the beaten tracks. You must bend aside the branches of the underbrush, or lean down and peep between the blackberry briars through the tall grasses and across the thick moss. Under the shaded leaves of the plants, in holes in the ground and tree-trunks, in the decaying bark of stumps, in the curl and twist of the roots that coil on the ground like serpents, there is an active, multi-form life by day and by night, full of joys and dangers, struggles and sorrows and pleasures.

Maya divined only a little of this as she flew low between the dark-brown trunks under the leafy roof of green. She followed a narrow trail in the grass, which made a clear path through thicket and clearing.

After a long stretch the woods opened their columned and over-arched portals; before Ma-ya's eyes lay a wide field of grain in the golden sunshine. Butterfly-weed flamed on the grassy borders. She alighted on the branch of a birch-tree at the edge of the field and gazed upon the sea of gold that spread out endlessly in the tranquillity of the placid day. It rippled softly under the shy summer breeze, which blew gen-tly so as not to disturb the peace of the lovely world.

Under the birch-tree a few small brown but-terflies, using the butterfly-weed for corners, were playing puss-in-the-corner, a favorite game with butterfly-children. Maya watched them a while.

"It must be lots of fun," she thought, "and the children in the hive might be taught to play it, too. The cells would do for corners.— But Cas-sandra, I suppose, wouldn't permit it. She's so strict."

Ah, now Maya felt sad again. Because she had
thought of home. And she was about to drift off
into homesick revery when she heard someone
beside her say:

"Good morning. You're a beast, it seems to
me."

Maya turned with a start.

"No," she said, "decidedly not."

There sitting on her leaf was a little polished
terra-cotta half-sphere with seven black dots on
its cupola of a back, a minute black head and
bright little eyes. Peeping from under the dotted
dome and supporting it as best they could Maya
detected thin legs fine as threads. In spite of his
queer figure, she somehow took a great liking to
the stout little fellow; he had distinct charm.

"May I ask who you are? I myself am Maya of
the nation of bees."

"Do you mean to insult me? You have no reason to."

"But why should I? I don't know you, really I don't."

Maya was quite upset.

"It's easy to *say* you don't know me.— Well, I'll jog your memory. Count."

And the little rotundity began to wheel round slowly.

"You mean I'm to count your dots?"

"Yes, if you please."

"Seven," said Maya.

"Well?— Well? You still don't know. All right then, I'll tell you. I'm called exactly according to what you counted. The scientific name of our family is Septempunctata. *Septem* is Latin for seven, *punctata* is Latin for dots, points, you see. Our common name is ladybird, my own name is Alois, I am a poet by profession. You know our common name, of course."

Maya, afraid of hurting Alois' feelings, didn't dare to say no.

"Oh," said he, "I live by the sunshine, by the peace of the day, and by the love of mankind."

"But don't you eat, too?" asked Maya, quite astonished.
깜짝 놀라다

"Of course. Plant-lice. Don't you?"
진딧물

"No. That would be—that is...."

"Is what? Is what?"

"Not—usual," said Maya shyly.
수줍게, 조심스럽게

"Of course, of course!" cried Alois, trying
~하려고 하다
to raise one shoulder, but not succeeding,
어깨를 으쓱하다   성공하다
on account of the firm set of his dome. "As a
딱딱한
bourgeoise you would, of course, do only what
부르주아, 물질만능주의적인, 속물적인
is usual. We poets would not get very far that
way.— Have you time?"
시간 있어요?

"Why, yes," said Maya.

"Then I'll recite you one of my poems. Sit
암송[낭송/낭독]하다   시
real still and close your eyes, so that nothing
distracts your attention. The poem is called
집중이 안 되게 하다. (주의를) 딴 데로 돌리다
Man's Finger, and is about a personal experi-
손가락   개인적인 경험
ence. Are you listening?"

"Yes, to every word."

"Well, then:

"'Since you did not do me wrong,

That you found me, doesn't matter.

You are rounded, you are long;

Up above you wear a flatter,

Pointed, polished sheath or platter

Which you move as swift as light,

But below you're fastened tight!'"

"Well?" asked Alois after a short pause. There were tears in his eyes and a quaver in his voice.

"*Man's Finger* gripped me very hard," replied Maya in some embarrassment. She really knew much lovelier poems.

"How do you find the form?" Alois questioned with a smile of fine melancholy. He seemed to be overwhelmed by the effect he had produced.

"Long and round. You yourself said so in the poem."

"I mean the artistic form, the form of my verse."

(시의) 연

"Oh—oh, yes. Yes, I thought it was very good."

"It is, isn't it!" cried Alois. "What you mean to say is that *Man's Finger* may be ranked among

(등급, 순위를) 차지하다

the best poems you know of, and one must go way back in literature before one comes across

거슬러 올라가다   문학

anything like it. The prime requisite in art is

제일요건

that it should contain something new, which is

포함하다, 담다

what most poets forget. And bigness, too. Don't

잊어버리다   크기, 치수

you agree with me?"

~에 동의하다

"Certainly," said Maya, "I think...."

"The firm belief you express in my impor-

확고한 믿음   표현하다   중요성

tance as a poet really overwhelms me. I thank

(격한 감정이) 휩싸다[압도하다]

you.— But I must be going now, for solitude is

(즐거운) 고독

the poet's pride. Farewell."

자랑, 자부심

"Farewell," echoed Maya, who really didn't

정말로

know just what the little fellow had been after.

…을 추구하다, …을 찾다

"Well," she thought, "*he* knows. Perhaps he's

아마

not full grown yet; he certainly isn't large."

완전히 자란   아직   분명히, 틀림없이   큰

She looked after him, as he hastened up the branch. His wee legs were scarcely visible; he looked as though he were moving on low rollers.

Maya turned her gaze away, back to the golden field of grain over which the butterflies were playing. The field and the butterflies gave her ever so much more pleasure than the poetry of Alois, ladybird and poet.

13

THE FORTRESS

How happily the day had begun and how miserably it was to end! Before the horror swept upon her, Maya had formed a very remarkable acquaintance. It was in the afternoon near a big old water-butt. She was sitting amid the scented elder blossoms, which lay mirrored in the placid dark surface of the butt, and a robin redbreast was warbling overhead, so sweetly and merrily that Maya thought it was a shame, a crying shame that she, a bee, could not make friends with the charming songsters. The trouble was, they were too big and ate you up.

행복하게 · 시작하다 (BEGIN의 과거분사) · 비참하게, 끔찍하게 · 참혹한 경험 · 휘몰아치다 · 놀랄 만한, 놀라운, 주목할 만한 · 빗물 받는 통 · ~속에 · 향기가 나다[풍기다] · 잔잔한 · 표면 · 울새 · 지저귀는, 노래하는 · 즐겁게 · 애석한[딱한/아쉬운] 일 · 친구가 되다 · 매력적인

She had hidden herself in the heart of the
elder blossoms and was listening and blinking
under the pointed darts of the sunlight, when
she heard someone beside her sigh.

Turning round she saw—well, now it really
was the strangest of all the strange creatures
she had ever met. It must have had at least a
hundred legs along each side of its body—so she
thought at first glance. It was about three times
her size, and slim, low, and wingless.

"For goodness sake! Mercy on me!" Maya was
quite startled. "You must certainly be able to
run!"

The stranger gave her a pondering look.

"I doubt it," he said. "I doubt it. There's room
for improvement. I have too many legs. You
see, before all my legs can be set in motion, too
much time is lost. I didn't use to realize this, and
often wished I had a few more legs. But God's
will be done.— Who are you?"

Maya introduced herself. The other one nodded and moved some of his legs.

자기소개를 하다 / 고개를 끄덕이다 / 움직이다

"I am Thomas of the family of millepeds. We are an old race, and we arouse admiration and astonishment in all parts of the globe. No other animals can boast anything like our number of legs. Eight is *their* limit, so far as I know."

노래기(지네처럼 생긴 절지동물) / 가계, 혈통: 명문 출신 / 흠모를 받다: 감탄을 자아내다 / 경탄, 놀라움 / 뽐내다, 자랑하다 / 한계(점), 한도

"You are tremendously interesting. And your color is so queer. Have you got a family?"

엄청나게, 굉장히 / 기묘한, 괴상한

"Why, no! Why should I? What good would a family do me? We millepeds crawl out of our eggs; that's all. If *we* can't stand on our own feet, who should?"

…에서 기어 나오다

"For one thing," said Thomas after a pause, "for one thing I doubt whether you have chosen a good place to rest in. Don't you know what's over there in the big willow?"

조금 있다가 / ~인지 아닌지 / 고르다, 선택하다 / 버드나무

"No."

"You see! I doubted right away if you knew. The city of the hornets is over there."

방금: 곧바로, 즉시 / 말벌

170

Maya turned deathly white and nearly fell

사색이 되다: 죽은 사람처럼 하얗게 질리다

off the elder blossoms. There, showing clear

뚜렷이 보이다

against the green, she saw the brown walls of

벽

the fortress. She almost stopped breathing.

요새   거의 숨이 멈추다

"I must fly away," she cried.

Too late! Behind her sounded a loud, mean

늦은   ~의 뒤에서   커다란   비열한, 상스러운

laugh. At the same moment the little bee felt

동시에, 같은 순간에

herself caught by the neck, so violently that she

목을 잡히다   격렬하게, 맹렬히: 끔찍하게

thought her joints were broken.

관절   부러지다

It was a laugh she would never forget, like

a vile taunt out of hellish darkness. Mingling

극도로 불쾌한[나쁜] 비웃음[조롱] 지독히 기분 나쁜: 지옥 같은   섞이다, 어우러지다

with it was another gruesome sound, the awful

섬뜩한, 소름끼치는   끔찍한, 지독한

clanking of armor.

철거덕거리는   갑옷

Thomas let go with all his legs at once and

즉시

tumbled head over heels through the branches

굴러 떨어지다

into the water-butt.

빗물받이 통

"Let go!" cried Maya. "Let me go! Or I'll sting

침을 쏘다

you in your heart."

"In my heart right away? Very brave. But

용감한

there's time for that later."

나중에

Maya went into a fury. Summoning all her
격노하다, 노발대발하다   소환하다, 불러내다
strength, she twisted herself around, uttered her
(입으로 어떤 소리를) 내다
shrill battle-cry, and directed her sting against
새된, 날카로운   (전쟁터에서의) 함성
the middle of the hornet's breast.
말벌의 가슴 한가운데
To her amazement and horror, the sting,
정말 놀랍고도 무섭게도   침
instead of piercing his breast, swerved on the
~를 뚫는 대신에   방향을 바꾸다[틀다]
surface. The brigand's armor was impervious.
표면   도둑, 산적   통과시키지 않는, 불침투성의
Wrath gleamed in his eyes.
(극도의) 분노, 노여움
"I could bite your head off, little one, to
(이빨로) 물다[베어 물다]
punish you for your impudence. And I would,
…때문에 벌주다   뻔뻔스러움, 몰염치; 건방짐, 무례함
too, I would indeed, but for our queen. She
정말로
prefers fresh bees to dead carcasses. So a good
~을 더 좋아하다   (큰 동물의) 시체; (식용으로 쓸) 죽은 동물
soldier saves a juicy morsel like you to bring to
(음식의) 작은 양[조각]
her alive."

The hornet, with Maya still in his grip, rose
꽉 붙잡음, 움켜쥠
into the air and made directly for the fortress.
곧장, 곧바로
"This is too awful," thought the poor little bee.
끔찍한, 무시무시한
"No one can stand this."
견뎌내다, 이겨내다
She fainted.
기절하다
When she came to her senses, she found her-
정신을 차리다
self in half darkness, in a sultry dusk permeated
무더운, 후텁지근한   스며들다, 퍼지다

172

by a horrid, pungent smell. Slowly everything
진저리나는, 지독한　(맛, 냄새가) 톡 쏘는 듯한[몹시 자극적인]
came back to her. A great paralyzing sadness
마비시키는, 무력하게 만드는
settled in her heart. She wanted to cry: the tears
refused to come.
거절하다, 거부하다

Through the walls of her prison she caught
벽을 통해서　　　　　　　　　감옥
the distinct sound of voices, and soon she
뚜렷한, 분명한　　　　　　　　곧
noticed that a little light filtered through a nar-
알아차리다, 주목하다　　　　(빛이나 소리가) 새어[스며] 들어오다
row chink. The hornets make their walls, not of
(빛이 새어드는) 틈
wax like the bees, but of a dry mass resembling
닮은, 비슷한
porous grey paper.

Again she heard voices on the other side of
the wall. Impelled by mortal fear, she crept up
…해야만 하게 하다　언젠가는 반드시 죽는　　기어올라가다
to the chink and peeped through.
틈　　　~ 틈으로 엿보다
What she saw was a vast hall crowded with
어마어마하게 큰　　모여들다
hornets and magnificently illuminated by a
장대하게, 장려하여, 화려하게　(…에 불을) 비추다
number of captive glow-worms. Enthroned in
사로잡힌, 억류된　반딧불이 비슷한 곤충　왕좌에 앉다
their midst sat the queen, who seemed to be
holding an important council. Maya caught ev-
중요한 회의
ery word that was said.

Then Maya heard the queen say:

"Very well, we shall abide by the arrange-
ments we have made. To-morrow, one hour
before dawn, the warriors will assemble and
sally forth to the attack on the city of the bees
in the castle park. The hive is to be plundered
and as many prisoners taken as possible. He
who captures Queen Helen VIII and brings her
to me alive will be dubbed a knight. Go forth
and be brave and victorious and bring back rich
booty.— The meeting is herewith adjourned.
Sleep well, my warriors. I bid you good-night."

The queen-hornet rose from her throne and
left the hall accompanied by her body-guard.

Maya nearly cried out loud.

"My country!" she sobbed, "my bees, my dear,
dear bees!"

She pressed her hands to her mouth to keep
herself from screaming. She was in the depths
of despair.

"Oh, would that I had died before I heard
this. No one will warn my people. They will be

attacked in their sleep and massacred. O God,
공격하다   대학살하다
perform a miracle, help me, help me and my
기적을 일으키다[행하다]
people. Our need is great!"

In the hall the glow-worms were put out and
devoured. Gradually the fortress was wrapped
           천천히, 점차적으로   요새
in a hush. Maya seemed to have been forgotten. A faint twilight crept into her cell, and she
      희미한, 어스름한
thought she caught the strumming of the crick-
                          (기타 같은 것을) 치는
ets' night song outside.— Was anything more
horrible than this dungeon with its carcasses
                        지하 감옥
strewn on the ground!
흩어지다, 흩뿌려져 있다 (STREW의 과거분사)

14

THE SENTINEL

Soon, however, the little bee's despair yielded to a definite resolve. It was as though she once more called to mind that she was a bee.

"Here I am weeping and wailing," she thought, "as if I had no brains and as if I were a weakling. Oh, I'm not much of an honor to my people and my queen. They are in danger. I am doomed anyhow. So since death is certain one way or another, I may as well be proud and brave and do everything I can to try to save them."

Maya began to widen the chink through
넓히다   벽의 틈
which she had peeped into the hall. It was easy
엿보다   쉬운
to bite away the brittle stuff of the partition,
깨물다   잘 부러지는 물질   칸막이
though it took some time before the opening

was large enough to admit her body.
충분히   들어가게 하다, 입장을 허락하다

At length, in the full knowledge that discovery
드디어, 한참 있다가   발견
would cost her her life, she squeezed through
~을 값으로 치르다   간신히 지나가다
into the hall. From remote depths of the fortress

echoed the sound of loud snoring.
코고는 소리

The hall lay in a subdued blue light that found
부드러운, 은은한
its way in through the distant entrance.
(거리가) 먼   출입구

"The moonlight!" Maya said to herself. She

began to creep cautiously toward the exit, cow-
조심스럽게   ~쪽으로, ~을 향하여
ering close in the deep shadows of the walls,
그림자
until she reached the high, narrow passageway
닿다, 도달하다   좁은   복도
that led from the hall to the opening through

which the light shone. She heaved a deep sigh.
크게 한숨 등을 내쉬다
Far, far away glimmered a star.

"Liberty!" she thought.

But there in the shadow of the doorway stood
출입구
a sentinel leaning against a column.
보초병, 감시병

Maya stood still, rooted to the spot. Vanished all her hopes. Gone the chance of escape. There was no getting by that formidable figure. What was she to do? Best go back where she had come from.

But the sight of the giant in the doorway held her in a spell. He seemed to be lost in revery. He stood gazing out upon the moon-washed landscape, his head tilted slightly forward, his chin propped on his hand. How his golden cuirass gleamed in the moonlight! Something in the way he stood there stirred the little bee's emotions.

Little Maya quite forgot that this man was her enemy. Ah, how often the same thing had happened to her—that the goodness of her heart and her delight in beauty made her lose all sense of danger.

A golden dart of light shot from the bandit's helmet. He must have turned his head.

"My God," whispered Maya, "this is the end of me!"

But the sentinel said quietly:

"Just come here, child."

"What!" cried Maya. "You saw me?"

"All the time, child. You bit a hole through the wall, then you crept along—crept along—tucking yourself very neatly into the dark places—until you reached the spot where you're standing. Then you saw me, and you lost heart. Am I right?"

"Yes," said Maya, "quite right."

"What are you doing here?" he asked good-humoredly.

"I'd like to get out," she answered. "And I'm not afraid. I was just startled. You looked so strong and handsome, and your armor shone so. Now I'll fight you."

The sentinel, slightly astonished, leaned for-ward, and looked at Maya and smiled. It was not an ugly smile, and Maya experienced an entirely new feeling: the young warrior's smile seemed to exercise a mysterious power over her heart.

"No, little one," he said almost tenderly, "you and I won't fight. You bees belong to a powerful nation, but man for man we hornets are stronger. To do single battle with a bee would be beneath our dignity. If you like you may stay here a little while and chat. But only a little while. Soon I'll have to wake the soldiers up; then, back to your cell you must go."

"I have always heard bad things about hornets. But you are not bad. I can't believe you're bad."

The warrior looked at Maya.

"There are good people and bad people everywhere," he said, gravely. "But you mustn't forget we are your enemies, and shall always remain your enemies."

"You are powerful. If you want to, you can put me back in my cell, and I'll have to die. But you can also set me free—if you want to."

"You are right," he said. "I can. My people and my queen have entrusted me with this power. My orders are that no bee who has set foot in

this fortress shall leave it alive. I shall keep faith
with my people."

After a pause he added softly as if to himself:
"I have learned by bitter experience how faith-
lessness can hurt—when Loveydear forsook
me...."

Loveydear—why, she knew Loveydear—the
beautiful dragon-fly who lived at the lakeside
among the waterlilies.

"Who is Loveydear, if I may ask?"

"Never mind, little one. She's not your affair,
and she's lost to me forever. I shall never find
her again."

"I know Miss Loveydear." Maya forced herself to put the utmost indifference into her tone.
"She belongs to the family of dragon-flies and
she's the loveliest lady of all."

A tremendous change came over the warrior.
He seemed to have forgotten where he was. He
leapt over to Maya's sides as if blown by a violent gust.

"What! You know Loveydear? Tell me where she is. Tell me, right away."

"No."

Maya spoke quietly and firmly; she glowed with secret delight.

"I'll bite your head off if you don't tell."

The warrior drew dangerously close.

"It will be bitten off anyhow. Go ahead. I shan't betray the lovely dragon-fly. She's a close friend of mine.... You want to imprison her."

The warrior breathed hard. In the gathering dawn Maya could see that his forehead was pale and his eyes tragic with the inner struggle he was waging.

"Good God!" he said wildly. "It's time to rouse the soldiers.— No, no, little bee, I don't want to harm Loveydear. I love her, more dearly than my life. Tell me where I shall find her again."

Maya was clever. She purposely hesitated before she said:

"But I love my life."

182

"If you tell me where Loveydear lives, I'll set you free. You can fly wherever you want."

"Will you keep your word?"

"My word of honor as a brigand," said the sentinel proudly.

"Very well," Maya said, "I believe you. Listen, then. Do you know the ancient linden-trees near the castle? Beyond them lies one meadow after another, and finally comes a big lake. In a cove at the south end where the brook empties into the lake the waterlilies lie spread out on the water in the sunlight. Near them, in the rushes, is where Loveydear lives. You'll find her there every day at noon when the sun is high in the heavens."

"You're telling the truth," he said softly and groaned, whether from joy or pain it was impossible to tell. "She told me she wanted to go where there were floating white flowers. Those must be the flowers you speak of. Fly away, then. I thank you."

And actually he stepped aside from the entrance.

Day was breaking.

"A brigand keeps his word," he said.

Not knowing that Maya had overheard the deliberations in the council chamber, he told himself that one small bee more or less made little difference. Weren't there hundreds of others?

"Good-by," cried Maya, breathless with haste, and flew off without a word of thanks.

As a matter of fact, there was no time to spare.

15

THE WARNING

Little Maya summoned every bit of strength
and will power she had left. Like a bullet
shot from the muzzle of a gun (bees can fly faster than most insects), she darted through the
purpling dawn in a lightning beeline for the
woods, where she knew she would be safe for
the moment and could hide herself away should
the hornet regret having let her go and follow in
pursuit.

It was not easy for her to find her way over
the woods. Long before she had ceased to observe landmarks as did the other bees, who had

great distances to come back with their loads of nectar. She felt she had never flown as high before, the cold hurt, and she could scarcely distinguish the objects below.

"What can I go by?" she thought. "No one thing stands out. I shan't be able to reach my people and help them. Oh, oh! And here I had a chance to atone for my desertion. What shall I do? What shall I do?"

Suddenly some secret force steered her in a certain direction.

"*What* is pushing and pulling me? It must be homesickness guiding me back to my country."

She gave herself up to the instinct and flew swiftly on. Soon, in the distance, looking like grey domes in the dim light of the dawn, showed the mighty lindens of the castle park. She exclaimed with delight. She knew where she was. She dropped closer to the earth.

On the flying-board, two sentinels blocked the entrance and laid hands upon her. Maya was too breathless to utter a syllable, and the sentinels threatened to kill her.

"Stand back!" cried one sentinel, thrusting her roughly away. "What's the matter with you! If you don't leave this instant, you'll die.— Did you ever!"

He turned to the other sentinel.

"Have you ever seen the like, and before day-time too?"

Now Maya pronounced the password by which all the bees knew one another. The sentinels instantly released her.

"What!" they cried. "You are one of us, and we don't know you?"

"Let me get to the queen," groaned the little bee. "Right away, quick! We are in terrible danger."

The sentinels still hesitated. They couldn't grasp the situation.

"The queen may not be awakened before sunrise," said the one.

"Then," Maya screamed, her voice rising to a passionate yell such as the sentinels had prob-ably never heard from a bee before, "then the queen will never wake up alive. Death is follow-ing at my heels. Take me to the queen! Take me to the queen, I say!"

Her voice was so wild and wrathful that the sentinels were frightened, and obeyed.

The three hurried together through the warm, well-known streets and corridors. Maya recognized everything, and for all her excite-ment and the tremendous need for haste, her heart quivered with sweet melancholy at the sight of the dear familiar scenes.

The first wax-generators were already up. Here and there a little head thrust itself out curiously from the openings. The news of the incident traveled quickly.

Two officers emerged from the private cham-bers. Maya recognized them instantly. In sol-emn silence, without a word to her, they took their posts, one on each side of the doorway: the queen would soon appear.

She came without her court, attended only by her aide and two ladies-in-waiting. She hurried straight over to Maya. When she saw what a state the child was in, the severe expression on her face relaxed a little.

"You have come with an important message? Who are you?"

Maya could not speak at once. Finally she managed to frame two words:

"The hornets!"

The queen turned pale. But her composure was unshaken, and Maya was somewhat calmed.

"Almighty queen!" she cried. "Forgive me for not respecting the duties I owe Your Majesty. Later I will tell you everything I have done. I repent. With my whole heart I repent.— Just a little while ago, as by a miracle, I escaped from the fortress of the hornets, and the last I heard was that they were planning to attack and plunder our kingdom at dawn."

The wild dismay that the little bee's words
(실망, 경악)
produced was indescribable. The ladies-in-
(이루 말할 수 없다)   (시녀)
waiting set up a loud wail, the officers at the
(울음을 터뜨리다)   (장교)
door turned pale and made as if to dash off and
(뛰쳐나가다)
sound the alarm, the aide said: "Good God!" and
(보좌관)   (맙소사)
wheeled completely round, because he wanted
(완전히)
to see on all sides at once.

As for the queen, it was really extraordinary to
(보기 드문, 비범한; 대단한)
see with what composure, what resourcefulness
(마음의) 평정   지모[계략]가 풍부함
she received the dreadful news. She drew her-
받다, 받아들이다   끔찍한   ~를 일으켜세우다
self up, and there was something in her attitude
(정신적인) 태도[자세]
that both intimidated and inspired endless
겁을 주다, 위협하다   고무하다, 격려하다
confidence. Little Maya was awed. Never, she
신뢰, 자신감   외경심에 휩싸인[사로잡힌]
felt, had she witnessed anything so superior. It
보다, 목격하다   (…보다 더) 우수한[우월한]
was like a great, magnificent event in itself.
참으로 아름다운[감명 깊은/훌륭한]
The queen beckoned the officers to her side
(오라고) 손짓하다. (손짓으로) 부르다
and uttered a few rapid sentences aloud.
(속도가) 빠른
"O my queen!" said Maya.

The queen inclined her head to the little bee,
~쪽으로 기울다[기울어지게 하다]
who once again for a brief moment saw her

monarch's countenance beam upon her gently, lovingly.

"You have our thanks," she said. "You have saved us. No matter what your previous conduct may have been, you have made up for it a thousandfold.— But go, rest now, little girl, you look very miserable, and your hands are trembling."

She bent over and kissed the little bee on her forehead. Then she beckoned to the ladies-in-waiting and bade them see to Maya's rest and comfort.

Maya, stirred to the depths of her being, allowed herself to be led away. After this, life had nothing lovelier to offer. As in a dream she heard the loud, clear signals in the distance, saw the high dignitaries of state assemble around the royal chambers, heard a dull, far-echoing drone that shook the hive from roof to foundation.

"The soldiers! Our soldiers!" whispered the ladies-in-waiting at her side.

The last thing Maya heard in the little room where her companions put her to bed was the tramp of soldiers marching past her door and commands shouted in a blithe, resolute, ringing voice. Into her dreams, echoing as from a great distance, she carried the ancient song of the soldier-bees:

Sunlight, sunlight, golden sheen,
   By your glow our lives are lighted;
Bless our labors, bless our Queen,
   Let us always be united.

16

THE BATTLE

The kingdom of the bees was in a whirl of excitement. Not even in the days of the revolution had the turmoil been so great. The hive rumbled and roared. Every bee was fired by a holy wrath, a burning ardor to meet and fight the ancient enemy to the very last gasp. Yet there was no disorder or confusion. Marvelous the speed with which the regiments were mobilized, marvelous the way each soldier knew his duty and fell into his right place and took up his right work.

It was high time. At the queen's call for volun-

teers to defend the entrance, a number of bees
방어하다, 수비하다
offered themselves, and of these several had
(몇)몇의: 각각[각자]의
been sent out to see if the enemy was approach-
접근하다
ing. Two had now returned—whizzing dots—and
윙 하는 소리
reported that the hornets were drawing near.
보고하다

An awesome hush of expectancy fell upon
경탄할 만한, 어마어마한, 엄청난   기대
the hive. Soldiers in three closed ranks stood

lined up at the entrance, proud, pale, solemn,

composed. No one spoke. The silence of death
침묵, 고요
prevailed, except for the low commands of the
만연[팽배]하다   ~만 빼고, ~을 제외하고   명령
officers drawing up the reserves in the rear. The

hive seemed to be fast asleep.
깊은 잠에 빠진 것처럼 보이다
The only stir came from the doorway where

about a dozen wax-generators were at work in
밀랍을 만드는 일벌
feverish silence executing their orders to nar-
몹시 흥분한, 과열된   실행[수행]하다   좁히다
row the entrance with wax. As by a miracle, two

thick partitions of wax had already gone up,
두꺼운   칸막이
which even the strongest hornets could not bat-

ter down without great loss of time. The hole

had been reduced by almost half.
줄다, 좁아지다, 축소하다
The queen took up an elevated position in-

side the hive from which she was able to survey [살피다. 점검하다]
the battle. Her aides flew scurrying hither and [종종걸음을 치다. 총총[허둥지둥] 가다]
thither.

But when in the quiet of the morning an
ominous whirring was heard outside the hive, [불길한]
first softly, then louder and louder, and the
entrance darkened, and the whispering voices [어두워지다]
of the hornets, the most frightful robbers and [무서운, 끔찍한] [강도]
murderers in the insect world, penetrated into [살인자] [곤충] [뚫고 들어가다[침투하다]]
the hive, then the faces of the valiant little bees [용맹한: 단호한]
turned pale as if washed over by a drab light [생기 없는, 칙칙한]
falling upon their ranks. They gazed at one an- [응시하다]
other with eyes in which death sat waiting, and
those who were ranged at the entrance knew
full well that one moment more and all would
be over with them.

The queen's controlled voice came clear and [침착한]
tranquil from her place on high: [고요한, 평온한]
"Let the robbers enter one by one until I give [강도] [들어오다] [하나씩] [~까지]
orders to attack. Then those at the front throw [공격하다]
themselves upon the invaders a hundred at a

time, and the ranks behind cover the entrance.
In that way we shall divide up the enemy's
forces. Remember, you at the front, upon your
strength and endurance and bravery depends
the fate of the whole state. Have no fear; in
the dusk the enemy will not see right away
how well prepared we are, and he will enter
unsuspecting...."

She broke off. There, thrust through the
doorway, was the head of the first brigand. The
feelers played about, groping, cautious, the pin-
cers opened and closed. It was a blood-curdling
sight. Slowly the huge black-and-gold striped
body with its strong wings crept in after the
head. The light falling in from the outside drew
gleams from the warrior's cuirass.

Something like a quiver went through the
ranks of the bees, but the silence remained un-
broken.

The hornet withdrew quietly. Outside he
could be heard announcing:

"They're fast asleep. But the entrance is half walled up and there are no sentinels. I do not know whether to take this as a good or a bad sign."

"A good sign!" rang out. "Forward!"

At that two giants leapt in through the entrance side by side; after them, soundlessly, pressed a throng of striped, armed, gleaming warriors, awful to behold. Eight made their way into the hive.

Still no orders to attack from the queen. Was she dumb with horror, had her voice failed her? And the brigands, did they not see in the shadow, to right and left, the soldiers drawn up in close, glittering ranks ready for mortal combat...?

Now at last came the order from on high:

"In the name of eternal right, in the name of your queen, to the defense of the realm!"

At that a droning roar went up. Never before had the city been shaken by such a battle-cry.

Those of the assailants who had already
penetrated into the hive quickly realized that
they must make their way still deeper inward if
they were not to block up the entrance to their
comrades outside. And so the struggling knots
rolled farther and farther down the dark streets
and corridors.

How right the queen had been in her tactics!
No sooner was a bit of space at the entrance
cleared than the ranks in the rear leapt forward
to its defense. It was an old strategy, and a
dreadful one for the enemy.

When a hornet at the entrance gave signs of
exhaustion, the bees shammed the same, and
let him crawl in; but the instant the one behind
showed his head a great swarm of fresh soldiers
dashed up to defend the apparently unprotected
entrance, while the invader who had gone on
ahead would find himself, already wearied, suddenly confronted by glittering ranks of soldier-
bees who had not yet stirred a finger in battle.

Generally he succumbed to their superior numbers at the very first attack.

Gradually the din subsided. The loud calls of
the hornets on the outside met with no response
from the invaders within.

"They are all dead," said the leader of the
hornets grimly, and summoned the combatants
back from the entrance. Their numbers had
melted down to half.

"We have been betrayed," said the leader.
"The bees were prepared."

"Be quick!" he cried, laying the white petal of a
jasmine in the messenger's hand, "or the human
beings will soon come and we shall be lost. Tell
the bees we will go away and leave them in peace
forever if they will deliver up the prisoners."

The messenger rushed off. At the entrance
he waved his white signal and alighted on the
flying-board. The queen-bee was immediately
informed that an emissary was outside who
wanted to make terms, and she sent her aide to

parley with him. When he returned with his re-
port she sent back this reply:

"We will deliver up the dead if you want to
take them away. There are no prisoners. All of
your people who invaded our territory are dead.
Your promise never to return we do not believe.
You may come again, whenever you wish. You
will fare no better than you did to-day. And if
you want to go on with the battle we are ready
to fight to the last bee."

The leader of the hornets turned pale when
this message was delivered to him. He clenched
his fists, he fought with himself. Only too gladly
would he have yielded to the wishes of his
warriors who clamored for revenge. Reason
prevailed.

Turning to the messenger, he cried:

"Give us back our dead. We will withdraw."

A dead silence fell. The messenger flew off.
In gloomy silence the troop of hornets waited
on the silver-fir and saw the corpses of their

fallen warriors drop one by one to the earth.
떨어지다 / 하나씩

The sun arose upon a scene of endless desolation. Twenty-one slain, who had died a glorious death, made a heap in the grass under the city of the bees. Not a drop of honey, not a single prisoner had been taken by the enemy.
황량함, 적막함 / 영광스러운, 영예로운 / 무더기, 더미 / 꿀 한 방울

The hornets picked up their dead and flew away, the battle was over, the bees had conquered.
집어 들다[올리다] / 전투 / ~이 끝나다 / 이기다, 물리치다

But at what a cost! Everywhere lay fallen bodies, in the streets and corridors, in the dim places before the brooders and honey-cupboards. Sad was the work in the hive on that lovely morning of summer sunshine and scented blossoms. The dead had to be disposed of, the wounded had to be bandaged and nursed.
얼마나 값비싼 승리인가! / 어둑한, 흐릿한 / 인공 부화기: 산란방 / 꿀 창고 / 향기 나는 / ~을 없애다[처리하다] / 부상 당한 / 붕대를 감다 / 간호하다

But before the hour of noon had struck, the regular tasks were begun; for the bees neither celebrated their victory nor spent time mourning their dead. Each bee carried his pride and his grief locked quietly in his breast and went about his work.
규칙적인, 정기적인 / 어느 것도 …아니다 / 기념하다, 축하하다 / 승리 / 쓰다, 낭비하다 / 애도 / 자부심, 자긍심 / 슬픔 / 가슴

17

THE QUEEN'S FRIEND

he noise of battle awoke Maya out of a
brief sleep. She jumped up and straightway
wanted to dash out to help defend the city, but
soon realized that she was too weak to be of any
help.

A group of struggling combatants came roll-
ing toward her. One of them was a strong young
hornet, an officer, Maya judged by his badge,
who was defending himself unaided against an
overwhelming number of bees. The struggling
knot drew nearer. To Maya's horror it left one
dead bee after another in its wake.

But numbers finally told against the giant: whole clusters of bees, ready to die rather than let go, hung to his arms and legs and feelers, and their stings were beginning to pierce between the rings of his breast. Maya saw him drop down exhausted. Without cry or complaint, fighting to the very end, neither suing for mercy nor reviling his opponents, he went down to his brigand's death.

The bees left him and hurried back to the entrance to throw themselves anew into the conflict.

Maya's heart was beating stormily. She slipped over to the hornet. He lay curled up in the twilight, still breathing. She counted about twenty stings, most of them in the fore part of his body, leaving his golden armor quite whole and sound. Seeing he was still alive, she hurried away to bring water and honey—to cheer the dying man, she thought. But he shook his head and waived her off with his hand.

"I *take* what I want," he said proudly. "I don't care for gifts."

"Oh," said Maya, "I only thought you might be thirsty."

The young officer smiled at her, then said, not sadly, but with a strange earnestness:

"I must die."

"If there were only *some*thing I could do," she said, and burst into tears.

The dying hornet made no answer. He opened his eyes once again and heaved a deep breath—for the last time. Half an hour later he was thrown down into the grass outside the hive along with his dead comrades.

Little Maya never forgot what she had learned from this brief farewell. She knew now for all time that her enemies were beings like herself, loving life as she did and having to die a hard death without succor. She thought of the flower sprite who had told her of his rebirth when Nature sent forth her blossoms again in the spring;

and she longed to know whether the other creatures would, like the sprite, come back to the
light of life after they had died the death of the
earth.

A messenger now came and summoned her
to the queen's presence.

She found the full court assembled in the royal reception room. Her legs shook, she scarcely
dared to raise her eyes before her monarch
and so many dignitaries. A number of the officers of the queen's staff were missing, and the
gathering was unusually solemn. Yet a gleam of
exaltation seemed to light every brow—as if the
consciousness of triumph and new glory won
encircled everyone like an invisible halo.

The queen arose, made her way unattended
through the assemblage, went up to little Maya
and took her in her arms.

This Maya had never expected, not this. The
measure of her joy was full to overflowing; she
broke down and wept.

The bees were deeply stirred. There was not one among them who did not share Maya's happiness, who was not deeply grateful for the little bee's valiant deed.

Maya now had to tell her whole story. Everybody wanted to know how she had learned of the hornets' plans and how she had succeeded in breaking out of the awful prison from which no bee had ever before escaped.

So Maya told of all the remarkable things she had seen and heard, of Miss Loveydear with the glittering wings, of the grasshopper, of Thekla the spider, of Puck, and of how splendidly Bobbie had come to her rescue. When she told of the sprite and the human beings, it was so quiet in the hall that you could hear the generators in the back of the hive kneading the wax.

"Ah," said the queen, "who'd have thought the sprites were so lovely?"

She smiled to herself with a look of melancholy and longing, as people will who long for

beauty. And all the dignitaries smiled the same
smile.

"How did the song of the sprite go?" she
asked. "Say it again. I'd like to learn it by heart."
Maya repeated the song of the sprite.

My soul is that which breathes anew
From all of loveliness and grace;

And as it flows from God's own face,
It flows from his creations, too.

There was silence for a while. The only sound
was a restrained sobbing in the back of the
hall—probably someone thinking of a friend
who had been killed.

Maya went on with her story. When she came
to the hornets, the bees' eyes darkened and wid-
ened. Each imagined himself in the situation in
which one of their number had been, and quivered, and drew a deep breath.
"Awful," said the queen, "perfectly awful...."

The dignitaries murmured something to the same effect.

"And so," Maya ended, "I reached home. And I sue for your Majesty's pardon—a thousand times."

Oh, no one bore the little bee any ill will for having run away from the hive. You may imagine they did not.

The queen put her arm round Maya's neck.

"You did not forget your home and your people," she said kindly. "In your heart you were loyal. So we will be loyal to you. Henceforth you shall stay by my side and help me conduct the affairs of state. In that way, I think, your experiences, all the things you have learned, will be made to serve the greatest good of your people and your country."

Cheers of approval greeted the queen's words.

So ends the story of the adventures of Maya the bee. They say her work contributed greatly to the good and welfare of the nation, and she came to be highly respected and loved by her people. Sometimes on quiet evenings she went for a brief hour's conversation to Cassandra's peaceful little room, where the ancient dame lived now on pension honey. There Maya told the young bees, who listened to her eagerly, stories of the adventures which we have lived through with her.

☜ 나만의 리뷰 and 명문장

📖 나만의 리뷰 and 명문장

🛇 나만의 리뷰 and 명문장